I ONLY
SPIT IN
BROOKLYN

I ONLY SPIT IN BROOKLYN

RONN COSTABILE

BL BRIDGE
LOGOS

Newberry, FL 32669

Bridge Logos, Inc
Newberry, FL 32669

I Only Spit in Brooklyn
Breaking Free From the Underworld
by Ronn Costabile

Printed in the United States of America

Library of Congress Catalog Card Number: 2018931859

International Standard Book Number: 978-1-61036-990-9

Cover photo: James Maher Photography, New York City

Cover design: Cameron Toman | camerontoman1@gmail.com

Interior design: Kent Jensen | knsil.com

Scripture quotations marked (NIV) are taken from the Holy Bible, New International Version®, NIV®. Copyright ©1973, 1978, 1984, 2011 by Biblica, Inc. Used by permission of Zondervan. All rights reserved worldwide. www.zondervan.com The "NIV" and "New International Version" are trademarks registered in the United States Patent and Trademark Office by Biblica, Inc.

Scripture quotations marked (TLB) are taken from The Living Bible, copyright © 1971. Used by permission of Tyndale House Publishers, Inc., Carol Stream, Illinois 60188. All rights reserved.

DEDICATION

Dedicated to Susan Morrison Constable

Susan and I were birds of a feather. We both cheated death together numerous times. But Susan continued to live on the edge.

I thank her for giving me the best daughter anyone could ask for. Conceived in the heat of paralyzing addictions and dangers, Tiffani grew to be a wonderful mother and wife.

Thank you, Susan.

Also dedicated to Art and Eleanor Duble

Art and Eleanor saw something good in me when no one else could. They are gone now; yet they will remain in my heart as my father and mother forever.

FOREWORD

At a time when our nation is suffering from the worst plague of addiction in our history, here is a timely story of recovery and transformation out of the depths of drugs with all its effects. I've known Ronn for years, and to meet him you would never know he had such a past as he shares his life experiences in addiction. I highly recommend this book. It will inspire you, make you smile, or laugh at times; but more importantly it will help the reader find out that addiction does not have to be a life-sentence.

—Don Wilkerson
Co-Founder of Teen Challenge
and Times Square Church

PREFACE

Super Bowl Sunday, 1987

January 25, 1987 arrived, and it was about 11:00 a.m.. It was five hours before the kickoff of one of the most highly publicized Super Bowls to date—Super bowl XXI between the New York Giants and the Denver Broncos.

Pat Summerall and John Madden were on TV stirring up the viewers with their pre-game excitement. Kickoff was at 4:00 p.m., and I was about to open up the "Phones" to begin our bookmaking operation. But withdrawal symptoms were beginning their familiar ugly signs in me—sweating, jumping muscles, nausea, diarrhea.

I had just returned to the "office" that we temporarily rented on West 56th street in Manhattan after picking up my fix on 127th Street in Harlem. After getting inside I quickly cooked up and shot a hit of heroin so I could function. I had to be straight when I opened up the phones to high-end betters by noon.

And then the bets started pouring in.

$5,000 on the Giants plus 8½ points. $20,000 on the Giants plus 8½. $50,000 on the Giants plus 8½. The calls were relentless.

I then called our "man" in Vegas to check on the line. He screamed, "Lower the line, lower the line!"

I lowered the line to 8 points . . . then to 7½, as I tried to balance out the betting.

Then 3:00 p.m. arrived, and the monkey was on my back again. But this time it was King Kong, and I was out of control. I panicked as the phones kept ringing off the hook. Kickoff was only one hour away.

Out of my mind and against every rule in the mob's playbook, I took both phones off the hook for what I thought would be only a few moments so I could quickly cook up and shoot up another hit of heroin. I had to get straight. La famiglia would kill me if I could not function!

So I cooked up. I tied up. I shot up; . . . I overdosed.

TABLE OF CONTENTS

INTRODUCTION

I want to begin by saying that the seemingly derogatory and offensive title of this book is not meant to be in any way a smear or a slur against Brooklyn, New York. So *fuhgeddaboudit!* As a matter of fact, it's just the contrary, as you will see as this book progresses.

At one time Brooklyn may have been my nemesis, but in all actuality it is the only place where I feel at home. Besides, all my *goombahs* are there. And Brooklyn is where you can get pizza (I mean real pizza, ehhh) and cannolis that are off the charts—*bello magnifico dolce!*

> *There's no better feeling in the world than a warm pizza box on your lap.*
> —Kevin James

I am a New Yorker by birth. So for all you Brooklynites and New Yorkers who read this, relax! I am one of you.

But Brooklyn is where I and my ex-wife, Susan, had our meltdown as we dissolved into a hidden world that most human beings cannot begin to understand or even know exists.

It's the hidden world of the heroin addict, formerly only known as the world of the *junkie.*

There are things about this Underworld that only a junkie knows. We were invisible to the outside, *straight* world, not worth the trouble for them to strain their eyes to see. We were all around them, co-existing, but they were blind to our presence.

It was like we lived in another world, and had become so alienated from the people of earth, that it was as if we actually lived on a different planet. Only a sub-human race of people lived on our planet, and in real ways, we fed off each other.

The world of the addict is a selfish world of survival—a world where there is a thin line between life and death. For us, as well as all heroin addicts, it is a dog-eat-dog world—*survival of the fittest.*

We felt as if we were no longer part of the human race—being banned to *Never-never Land*—to the Underworld, where living in complete delusion became our norm.

We knew nothing else—remaining in the shadows, hidden there and living like vampires, only that we survived on heroin, not blood. Yet for some depraved reason, addicts are infatuated with the sight of blood which fueled that same powerful craving and drove us on day after day, hour by hour, to heroin.

We felt dirty, rejected, and devoid of any and all self-esteem; so we remained there in Never-never Land—there above and below the streets of Brooklyn, in the shooting galleries of Red Hook, in the Lower East Side, in Harlem, and anywhere else we could find our fix.

Wherever the killer-heroin was, and wherever the purest cocaine was, you would find us chasing it. Being "on a mission" was the popular street term for our pursuit. We were "chasing the bag" (that is, the $10 bag). We were "chasing poison" and "chasing green tape"—an identifying stamp we looked for on the $10 bags of heroin of the '70s and the '80s.

That was the world I lived in, and sadly, nothing has really changed in the underworld I just described except that the "junkies" are not called *junkies* any longer; they're referred to as the *Jet Set*. Also, the addicts are now much younger, and the heroin is now much more potent, much more affordable, and much more available.

Heroin will transform a human into a depraved creature with a total absence of moral restraint. I know, because that is what it did to me.

Susan and I had become involved in activities that were beyond our wildest imaginations as young innocent children and teens.

But unfortunately, that is not only what it did to Susan and I; the story is the same for over 200,000 heroin addicts throughout New York City. And most of them will not survive their addicted existence.

> *If you are an addict you are either using, clean, or dead. There is nothing in between.* —Gary, Ipswich, UK

The statistics stated in a blog entry by Stephanie Haney, entitled *The Opioid Epidemic's Biggest Culprit Isn't Just Heroin Anymore—It's Something Deadlier,* are sobering. Following are excerpts:

> *Drug overdose deaths have now become the leading cause of accidental deaths in the US with 52,404 fatalities in 2015, according to the American Society of Addiction Medicine; 33,091 of those deaths, which equates to more than six out of 10, involved an opioid.*

> *And it's getting worse. While official numbers aren't in yet, a New York Times preliminary report has the total number of drug overdose deaths for 2016 at more than 59,000, which it described as "the largest annual jump ever recorded in the United States."* . . .

> *Fentanyl itself is another popular option. The drug is "50 to 100 times more potent" than morphine according to the National Institute on Drug Abuse. Oftentimes, drug users don't realize they aren't getting quite what they bargained for until it's too late.* —Stephanie Haney August 22, 2017

I escaped death and found ultimate victory and restoration, but like so many other addicts my ex-wife Susan continued to flirt with death and *date the demon.*

Today, I tell everyone the same thing. I tell them the truth—that there is no easy way out of an addiction, but there is a way out.

ONE WAY OUT

As far as I am concerned (and I lived through this addiction), there is only one true way to complete freedom over heroin. And I'm not talking about drug maintenance, or sponsors, or medications, or programs.

There is a place for all those things. But what I'm talking about is "heart" freedom. The street confession of "once an addict always an addict" is not an accurate statement. But if that is what you believe, then it will be true for you, and you will never be free from heroin's influence, powerful grip, or control.

I liken a heroin addiction to a fish who has swallowed a hook.

If you are fishermen, you know it's *curtains* for any fish that has swallowed the hook. While a hook can be removed from a fish's mouth, there is no easy way to remove a hook when it's been swallowed. Clearly, in such cases the hook cannot usually be removed without killing the fish. And even if the fish survives to be thrown back into the water, the hook will remain embedded throughout the fish's shortened lifespan, and it will cripple its ability to function normally.

Like a fish swallowing a steel hook, when a drug abuser *swallows the hook*, there is no natural, easy way for it to be removed. However, I am a living testimony to the fact it can be removed . . . permanently . . . but only in one amazing way.

An addict—regardless of gender—does not have to go through a shortened life experiencing no quality-of-life and being a slave to methadone maintenance, suboxone, or other *legally* prescribed addictive opiate substitutes.

And my life's story testifies to the fact that addicts can receive such freedom from drugs that, once free, there is no longer a need to fear that "The Hook"—the demon of heroin—might snag them again at some point in their lives.

—Ronn

Myself, son Ron Jr., and baby daughter Tiffani in Staten Island at the height of my heroin addiction

CHAPTER 1

GRAPES AND ZEPPOLES

Although most of the years of my struggle with heroin and cocaine were spent in the Borough of Brooklyn in New York City, my story does not begin there. For all intents and purposes my departure from reality began in a city named Newark—Newark New Jersey that is. So as I begin to tell you about my journey in life, let's go back to the very beginning. Let's go back to my early developmental years—the important formative years of my youth.

It has been said that 85% of our adult behavioral patterns and character is fixed by the time we enter into grade school at approximately six years of age.

As I go back in my memory I can clearly remember certain painful words that shook my little world and began creating a very confused young child.

I started out as a little, innocent boy who loved to catch butterflies and collect insects and bees (ouch!). I loved to fish, and I ate everything I caught in the lakes—sunfish, eels, and every ugly thing that I thought might hopefully be edible. Basically, I did all the simple things that a little boy likes to do.

I was born in Rockville Center (Oceanside), Long Island, and lived with my parents in a modest, quiet neighborhood in Baldwin. No doubt we looked like the perfect little family, but before I was five years old my parents had separated and then divorced. My mother moved us to Jersey (a true New Yorker always says "Jersey"), where I was raised and schooled as a pre-teen and teenager. My father remained in our Baldwin, Long Island home.

So most of the early years of my life we lived in a city named Asbury Park, where my mother had settled after the divorce in a predominantly Italian neighborhood. It was there that I formed my early views of life and norms.

Since this was a predominantly Italian neighborhood it was no surprise that my closest friends, a "second family", so to say, who lived a few houses down, were the Beradescos.

Oh, how Mama Mary B. could cook! I can still see the Zeppole bubbling in the oil on the stove. And I can still see all of us standing around waiting to sprinkle a little powdered sugar on them as Ms. Mary fished them out of that pot.

> *The trouble with eating Italian food is that 5 or 6 days later you're hungry again.* —George Miller

If we weren't eating Zeppole in the kitchen, we were back in their garden eating figs or sitting under the grape vines popping those succulent wine grapes out of their skins and into our mouths. My mouth is watering as I write—(yours too?).

You cannot eat a cluster of grapes at once, no. But grape by grape it's easy.   —Jacques Roumain

And if we weren't raiding Mama Mary's garden and her fruit trees, we were over at the lake trapping muskrats. We used to trap those little, furry, aggressive varmints for their skins (pelts), which we sold to furriers.

I remember in Butch's basement—Butchie B. that is, my first and best friend when we moved into the neighborhood from New York—you could see dozens of muskrat pelts being stretched and hung up for drying. Today we probably would be charged by an animal rights groups for cruelty to animals and indicted by the state.

It was a good, family-oriented neighborhood. Even the family of the popular Hollywood actor, Danny Devito, lived just around the corner from us on Bridge Street. I remember how many of the kids would go to the porch of his house hoping he was there in order to tease him. Kids can be brutal.

I was always teased about my somewhat large Italian nose. And Danny was teased for his height. Well, folks, check him out today. He may still be short in stature, but he certainly isn't short on cash.

It's not the size of the dog in the fight, it's the size of the fight in the dog.   —Mark Twain

It appeared that I had a good childhood, but there was always something missing in my life. And I never quite knew what that missing part was until one day when my first grade teacher asked me about my father. Her words were the painful words I previously mentioned remembering, and they shook my little, innocent world. I'll get to what she said in a moment.

I couldn't fully realize just how important a father was in the everyday life of a growing and developing little boy until many years later. But even then I knew something was missing. The vacuum in my life created by a missing father proved to build in me a lack of confidence, and that eventually caused me to choose many dangerous paths in life.

My mother was a sweetheart, but she was so passive and gullible. She really gave me little or no direction or training in life. Her little boy could do no wrong, and without doubt I became a mama's boy. Unlike my mother, my father was a disciplinarian. But he was not with me. I was with him only when I visited him. And that was not often or long enough.

I understand now that I didn't know who I was, or what I was, or what was expected of me as a developing young child. All I knew was that something was missing. And the state of confusion I lived in increased as I grew into a young man, then into manhood. (That is, if you could call it manhood.) The truth is, I was growing into a ticking time bomb.

I grew up in the 1960s, and back then the idea of a *complete* and traditional family unit was firmly intact. I don't want to minimize the value of family members today who are trying to do their best in less-than-ideal circumstances; but the truth is, back then it was unusual to see divorced couples, children with multiple mothers or fathers, pregnant teens, and visibly dysfunctional family lifestyles.

Unlike today, when dysfunctional families are the highlight of prime time television programs, the shows on TV back in the 50's & 60's featured families that were "complete". Families that always set an example of good moral values. *Father Knows Best* was the number one show in America. Well . . . if father knew best, then I was in big trouble.

I had no father living with me to confide in on a regular basis. He was in New York and I was in Jersey.

And now, more about my teacher:

I was six years old at the time. My teacher was Miss Mahoney, and I loved her even though she washed my mouth out with soap once or twice.

Oh yes, teachers washed mouths out with soap in public schools back in those days. Foul language had no place in the classroom. Ha, let a teacher try to wash out the mouth of a six-year-old today! The precious little boy or girl would probably pull out a 9mm Israeli Uzi and blow the teacher's brains out. And if the child didn't do it, the child's parents would. Things certainly are not like they used to be.

The task of teachers is to take a lot of live wires and see that they're are well grounded. —Unknown

I can still vividly remember the day Miss Mahoney asked me about my father. I was six-years old and in the first grade. She didn't mean any harm in asking me about him, and she just asked me a simple question. But it was one that really rocked my world as a little boy.

Miss Mahoney didn't try to draw attention to me. She just pulled me aside quietly and whispered in my ear, "Ronn, is your father dead?".

I'll never forget it. I immediately rose up in defense and said, "No! No! No! I have a father . . . I have a father. He is not dead, and he lives in Long Island. He's not dead. I have a father!"

I already felt different from all my friends, who lived in *complete* families. I already felt different from the other little boys. They had fathers who lived with them. They had fathers who cared enough to be around them and help raise them to one day be the kind of adults they should be. But not me. I had no male figure to play ball with as a little boy. I had no dad who showed me how to wrestle and develop a proper sense of responsible masculinity.

I answered Miss Mahoney truthfully. I did have a father, and he still lived in Long Island, where I was born. But since my mother couldn't drive, much less afford a car, it was difficult for me to see him frequently because of the distance. And even when

I had the opportunity to be with him it was difficult for him to speak much into my life under the circumstances of divorce and his remarriage. His new wife and my mother hissed at each other like Sarah and Hagar.

Nevertheless, my sister and I visited him via train sometimes; and he took the train to visit us occasionally, too. I remember his deep voice and his big Italian hands—they seemed as large as Yogi Berra's baseball mitt. To me, he was *Superman*.

My father was born in Calvanico, Italy, a community in the province of Salerno in the Campania region of southwestern Italy, forty-five minutes by car from Naples.

> *"You may have the universe if I may have Italy"*
>   —Giuseppe Verdi

His parents named him Aniello Costabile—pronounced *Co-sta-beu-la* (he was very fussy about properly pronouncing our name).

I remember my father motioning with his hands (as all Italians do, of course) to help him express the beauty of the pronunciation of our name. In my mind I still picture him moving his hands like the conductor of a symphony orchestra.

> *Question: What do you call an Italian with his hands in his pockets?*
> *Answer: Mute.*

He entered the United States through Ellis Island as a teenager. He was unable to speak a word of English at the time; and upon his entry into the United States his papers were stamped *WOP* (Without Papers).

WOP soon became a racial slur commonly directed at Italian immigrants. Others mocked Italians by interpreting the acronym as " Working On Pavement".

Needless to say, my father was a strong man who had to overcome the verbal abuse of the ugly prejudice that Italian immigrants were experiencing in those days.

Because of the prejudice shown against Italians, my father decided to change his name. Like many other Italians of that era who *Americanized* their names (Tony Bennett and Dean Martin among them) he changed his name to James Constable—a good, English-sounding name. He then worked hard to lose most of his accent as he mastered the English language. In fact, he never spoke to us in Italian. The only Italian I grew up with was street slang.

Like many other immigrants who lived in the 1930s, my father began to prosper as he pursued the *American Dream*. With hard work and determination he eventually rose in status and in the business world—so much so that he became a vice president in the Remington Rand corporation in New York City.

After the death of his first wife, my father married my mother, Ann. My mother was born in Bayonne, New Jersey. And from my earliest memories I can remember she was always boasting and swooning over Frank Sinatra.

She was an executive private secretary for the Holland American cruise line in Manhattan. The way I understand it, my mother found my father to be an irresistible *Italian Stallion*. My father was sixty-two years old (yes, 62 years old), and my beautiful mother was thirty-five when I was conceived. Hey you know what they say about 'a chip off the old block.'

> *"Amor, che a nullo amato amar perdona,*
> *Mi prese del costui piacer sì forte,*
> *Che, come vedi, ancor non m'abbandona."*
> *"Love, which pardons no beloved from loving,*
> *took me so strongly with delight in him*
> *That, as you see, it still abandons me not."*
>
> —Dante Alighieri

My father loved all his children, all seven of us. My brother Arnold (Jim) was the youngest until he lost his life in a smoky house fire in 2010.

I had brothers and sisters "from another mother" much older than I scattered in different states.

There was James, the oldest, then Matty and Robert, followed by Amabel and Arleen, then myself and Arnold (Jim). Arleen and I are from the same mother and are the only two surviving siblings.

My father was a good devoted husband and father. His first marriage ended with the death of his wife. His second marriage ended in divorce with my mother. And his third marriage was a good and lasting marriage which ended only with his death at age 93. (By the way, Arnold Jim was born after me to my father at age 66.) Look out for the Italian stallions!!

My life might have turned out much differently if my mother and father had stayed together. But looking back doesn't change those early painful memories.

Someone said, " Your past does not determine who you are; Your past prepares you for who you are to become".

CHAPTER 2

MY INFATUATION

As I already inferred, to me my father was a great man, and I definitely respected him. But I was afraid of him. However, I didn't fear him because he was abusive toward me. I think it was simply because I didn't know how to relate to a male authority figure in my life. I couldn't understand his strong disciplinary ways when we were together.

I understand now that while he was tough on the outside, he was gentle on the inside, as I believe most Italians are. And I remember some of the more tender moments when were together. I remember him taking those big hands, and to me huge fingers, and delicately strumming the strings on his beloved mandolin that he would play when I was with him.

I loved him dearly and hungered for a closer relationship with him, but it never developed. More and more I developed into a mama's boy who was firmly chained to his mother's apron strings.

Remember that every son had a mother
whose beloved son he was,
and every woman had a mother
whose beloved son she wasn't.

—Marge Piercy

As a mama's boy I was a frightened little boy on the inside who struggled to act tough around the other little neighborhood boys—who were truly tough. I didn't know how to fight and defend myself, and I didn't know how play well in organized sports. Nevertheless, I was very athletic and gave everything my best shot. (And I was, by the way, a street stick-ball champ!)

From a very young age I felt most comfortable around girls, and this is something that developed into a major problem as I grew into my teen years.

Although I had other, distant, brothers and sisters, I had only one other sibling who grew up with me in the same home, and that was one of my two sisters. My sister and I shared a bedroom. Actually, we lived in a one-bedroom house, so we had no choice but for all of us to share the only bedroom we had.

So I was in effect raised by both my mother and my older sister Arleen; and I slept in my mother's bed. I always slept with my mother. (Who wants to sleep with his sister?) I remember that even as I grew past 10 years of age I found myself always entangling my legs with my mother's legs in order to feel secure. She had to be there. I always had to touch her. I had to see her and be near her. She was the only one worthy of all my devotion in those early, insecure years.

I still vividly remember being about 9 years old and in Long Island on a visit to my father. There I was on Jones Beach, crying my eyes out on the scorching hot sand because I wanted my mother. And even in our home in Jersey, if she had gone out to shop and was gone for even only an hour, I could be found pacing up and down on our front porch, watching the cars, counting every one of them, and anxiously waiting until my uncle pulled up in his car to let her out at the curb. (As I said, she never had a driver's license. She did gain a permit though.)

Without my mother near I was, literally, completely dysfunctional throughout my preteen years. She had to be there. I always had to touch her. I had to see her. She was my "god" in those early years. There was no strong arm of a father there when I needed him.

Now I know most little boys are attached to their mothers, and vice-versa, but my dependency on mine was clearly abnormal. And it is easy for me to see that my need was born out of deep insecurities.

Nevertheless, as I grew into my teen years I did develop many friends and was not only accepted but became quite popular. However, I was clearly a follower masquerading as a leader among the neighborhood boys. But I covered my insecurities very well—faking leadership qualities whenever possible and hoping I never had to be put to the test.

As I said, I was well-liked by all my friends; but I became especially popular with many of the neighborhood "cuties." And no doubt it quickly became very evident to anyone watching that one of my main weaknesses in life would be those females in my world.

My strong interest in girls developed early, and this became clear when at the age of ten I *fell in love* with a girl named Marcy.

I know there are a lot of 8, 9, and 10-year-old boys who get crushes on neighborhood school girls at that age, but that was different. That was loooooooooove! And I mean I was in love big time. I was love sick. I was infatuated—mesmerized! And trust me, my early attraction and need for being with Marcy spelled big trouble for the future.

> *I'm so in love, every time I look at you my soul gets dizzy.*
>
> —Jaesse Tyler

My *Rolls Royce* (Schwinn bicycle) was all shined up and decked out with fox tails and mud flaps, flippers and flags, you name it; and I often hopped on it and rode many miles (yes, miles—no exaggeration) to visit her and to "socialize" (Rigggght) with her downstairs in her home. (She lived in a rich section of the Jersey Shore area.).

That went on for months, and her parents didn't seem to be too concerned about it until one day when I took a bold step. They thought it was a little strange when I showed up with a fancy ring to give to Marcy.

I purchased quite a fashionable ring for *my girl*. I bought the ring for $29.95 from the *J.J. Newberry* department store after collecting all my savings from shoveling snow out of people's driveways during the winter months. ($29.95 in those days was like $329.95 today!) I broke the bank for Marcy, my little Miss America, and my love. Wow! What a ten -year-old knockout she was—truly, a ten-year-old Angelina Jolie look-alike.

Then there came the day when my love affair with Marcy came to an abrupt end—and I emphasize *abrupt*—when her parents discovered me trying to pull a *slick willie* move on her while downstairs in their home. Her parents forbad me to see her or communicate any longer with her. They put a "parental restraining order" on me, so to speak. And needless to say, I was devastated. My ten-year-old heart was absolutely broken. I was devastated.

I don't believe my reactions to being separated from Marcy were normal for a boy ten years old. That first big breakup wasn't easy on me. But I eventually got over it and moved on (even though I continued to think a lot about her even into my teen years). However, I certainly didn't get over my problem with females that was developing and deepening day by day.

The truth is, Marcy may have been my first "love," but she wasn't the first girl I tried to put the *slick willie* move on. That actually came two years earlier in the basement of my own home at the ripe old age of eight. And that was followed by a number of unsuccessful attempts with little young ladies *under the boardwalk* if you know what I mean. (I didn't know a lot about what I was doing at that age, but I was determined to make a good sailor's attempt of it.)

From this you can see that in the very early years of my life the groundwork was being laid for me to live a pretty promiscuous lifestyle. Females literally were becoming the first of many *addictions* that plagued my life.

> *To my embarrassment, I was born in bed with a lady*
> —Wilson Mizner

CHAPTER 3

SEX IN THE CITY

As I grew toward some semblance of maturity, I also grew up believing that I was born on the *wrong side of the tracks*. So I was never college-minded because early on in life I was exposed to firm distinctions in status and what I believed were our destinies. There were the rich people, and there were the poor people; it was as simple as that. And through my ignorance, I believed that *poordom* was my lot in life.

> *That there should one man die ignorant who had capacity for knowledge, this I call a tragedy.* —Thomas Carlyle

I believed that college was for only the rich and famous—a certain class of people. It was not something for my social class to be concerned about or even considered. However, I did have a certain open mind about what the future could look like for me.

*I do not suggest that you should not have an **open mind**, particularly as you approach college. But don't keep your **mind so open** that your brains fall out.*   —William Bennett

Well, that is what eventually happened to me!

As I continued to grow up I actually developed some strong social relationships with the guys, but the inner-confidence I needed as a young man seemed to fall farther and farther away from me. As I continued to hide my insecurities I believe I could have ended up like a lot of other young men whose inner struggles, like mine, lead them to form homosexual relationships.

However, My Solution...**THE LADIES**.

It seems that I chose to lose my male insecurities by proving my manhood with the ladies. Spending more and more time with *the ladies* was my solution.

I gained confidence only through my relationships with girls. And quite honestly, building and taking advantage of those relationships came pretty easy for me since I was downright adorable, thank you very much. (And a look at my high school picture will prove it.)

As a young man I had dark, wavy, *Frankie Valli* hair. And I had blue-green Italian eyes that seemed to knock the socks off the ladies.

Why, I was so appealing to them that I literally had to dodge the streetlights at night. My dreamboat appearance took them back a step or two, and I took full advantage of it. I never had to pursue the ladies. They pursued me.

At the age of fifteen I was hanging around with older, seventeen-year-old guys who had driver's licenses and keys to cars. Not being able to drive was actually an advantage for me since I wound up in the back seats of the spacious cars of the '60s. The cars were huge back in those days, and there were lots of nights when I wound up with a girl in the spacious back seat of one of them at a drive-in theater. My favorite back seat was in an Oldsmobile 98.

Making out and having sex in the back seat at the drive-in theaters while the movie played became the week's main event for me, every week. Truthfully, I don't think I ever really watched a movie at the drive-in. As far as I was concerned the drive-in theater was strictly a place where you went to score with your girlfriends.

Of course beer was commonly being passed around as we caroused late into the nights. But I hated it. Actually, I hated all alcohol with the exception of wine. However, peer pressure caused me to force myself to drink some alcohol with my friends.

My body rejected alcohol at the time, and that was a good thing; but unfortunately I discovered soon enough that it did not hate or reject other forms of mind and body-altering substances. To the contrary, in time I would find myself craving them, and they would eventually become the *lady* in my life—but more about that later.

I was becoming quite a hunk in those days. However, I was nowhere near a *Hulk*. But I was certainly a hunk, albeit a skinny one. And at the manly age of sixteen, my eyes fell upon the most beautiful girl I had ever seen since Marcy. Looking back I can say it must have been like when David's eyes fell upon Bathsheba. I was overwhelmed. I was smitten.

Just as David had to have Bathsheba, Ronn had to have Joan. Joan put the Hollywood starlets to shame, and I'm not joking. Everyone wanted Joan, the fourteen-year-old beauty queen. But guess who wound up with the prize? Ahem . . . yours truly.

So here we go again. What felt like a storybook fantasy began when I was sixteen, and Joan, fourteen. Our relationship was pretty typical of many others in those days. There were the beer parties on the weekends and sex on the living-room rug (whenever her parents were out or sleeping) or in the back seat of a car at the drive-in.

I'll have more about us later.

Like me, none of the other members of my social clique was college minded, and most of us were brought up in what would be classified today as the low to lower-middle class.

My mother, my sister, and I lived on my mother's monthly alimony of $200, which obviously greatly limited us financially. So from an early age I had to work hard for any of the *things* I wanted. Nothing was given to me.

My first official position was an operator of the *kiddie rides* on the Asbury Park, New Jersey boardwalk when I was fourteen. And to make money throughout my pre-teen and early-teen years I shoveled snow, cut lawns, and worked with my cousin Sal, a handyman.

Regardless of how ignorant and irresponsible I might have been about some things, I diligently saved money to be sure to have a car by the time I was seventeen. Having a car was an important status symbol. A person became "cool" when driving his souped-up, pin-striped street racer through town. And being cool meant you were "somebody".

Also, as I got closer to driving age, I was getting tired of back-seat-sex, and I certainly couldn't afford motel-sex. So finding ways to make *fast money* became a priority to me.

As a teenager still struggling with my deep insecurities, I was desperately looking for an identity. I still didn't really know who I was or why I was alive. At that time neither parent was speaking into my life, and *the streets* were molding my character. So from the age of fourteen through the next three years I sought ways to make fast money.

> *Instant gratification takes too long.* —Carrie Fisher

As I said, the streets were molding my character; and my environment combined with my Italian DNA seemed to naturally introduce me to many ways to make fast money. Believe it or not, at the ripe, young age of fourteen I was handicapping the horses at Monmouth Park.

My friends and I were under-age for entering the track, so we snuck through the gate or hopped over the fence to get in. *Running Numbers* and betting on the horses became one of my passions, or should I say, one of my early addictions.

My friends and I were at the track every Saturday afternoon trying to turn $20 into $2,000. At the end of every week we took our earnings from our jobs to Monmouth Park with a false hope of becoming millionaires.

Gambling seemed to be a lucrative option to us since we had no thought of gaining an education to become a means to increase our wealth. Of course I found out over a period of years that no matter how good a handicapper a person is, he will never come out ahead in the long run. My poor choices always led me to betting on slow horses and fast women.

For some reason the frustration of losing—and I never liked losing at anything—only fueled a deeper passion for gambling. And eventually my gambling extended into the sports world, especially basketball since basketball was "daily action". No matter what the sport, though—from football to boxing, and from basketball to hockey—I had to have action. I had to gamble every day!

Gambling simply became for me the first of many addictions along the long road of ignorance. I studied the sports world seven days a week like a hungry predator, but regardless of my efforts, I never had that "millionaire" pay day.

CHAPTER 4

FANTASYLAND

I finally did it. I got my car, my first car! It was a 1958 Ford, and it was smoooooooooooth. It was pinstriped and all decked out. And it had a HUGE back seat!

Frankie Valli and the Four Seasons were topping the charts, and the era of the doo-wop singers was in full swing, especially if you were Italian. Let me tell you, we WOPS can doo-wop like nobody else.

> *Rock and roll music, if you like it, if you feel it, you can't help but move to it. That's what happens to me. I can't help it.*
> —Elvis Presley

I sang second tenor in two different doo-wop groups myself. And one of the groups was actually auditioned by ABC Records. We sang in local gigs. We sang most songs a cappella that was just sweeeeeet harmony! Our first group—all Italian by the way (if I named them all you would think it was a crime family)—was named *Patsy & the Prells*. I was a Prell. (Whatever that was I don't know, but it went along well with Patsy.)

The second group I was in was named *Granville Jones and the Uptones*. It was an Italian and black group, and it was the one that almost made it with ABC records. Granville was an incredible singer (and tailor, by the way). Sadly, however, he was killed at a young age in a freak accident, but I won't go into that here.

Nicky A., who headed another popular group in the area, was topping the local clubs (and still is) with his incredible falsetto voice, and we were cruising the circuit every night singing for the ladies.

As for me, little timid Ronn was coming out of his shell, and he had something to prove to both himself and the world. He wanted to prove that he was not a wimp and a mama's boy; he was both "game" and cool. Nevertheless, he continued to ignorantly deny and cover up his strong insecurities; and he continued to do so through women, sex, and gambling—and soon to follow . . . *drugs*.

> *Ignorance is the night of the mind, but a night without moon or star.*   —Confucius

Joan and I were together throughout that period. And when I was eighteen (Joan was sixteen) something new was introduced into the picture that our lives were painting:

Marijuana . . . "It was the '60s man!"

I and many of the other guys were already getting cheap highs on beer and cough medicine. Cough medicine was a real cheap high, even cheaper than the gutter wines *Wild Irish Rose* and *Night Train* (wow, that stuff was nasty rot gut). So we believed it was just harmless fun that was beginning when we came across marijuana.

To me, "weed" seemed to be the best discovery of the century. And if a person was chiefly ignorant—and I believe it has already been clearly established that I excelled in that category—that person was a prime target for being enticed to experiment with marijuana and fall in love with it.

> *To be ignorant of one's ignorance is the malady of the ignorant.*
> —Amos Bronson Alcott

Researchers are discovering now that there are those who are genetically marked with addictive personalities. All they need is a *trigger*. Well, all the ingredients for an addictive nature were there in me from my earliest memories. It was there, time and time again, just waiting for another trigger, some form of precipitating stress.

I was always under stress of one kind or another. I was a ticking time bomb; so when I tried a little weed, guess what happened? Right! BANG! My gun soon went off. BANG! The trigger was pulled. I quickly fell in love with being high on marijuana. She became my new lady. And what she could do for me was different from what I got from all the other ladies before her.

Marijuana brought to me something different. It was better than the cheap highs of the other substances. Marijuana brought me an escape from reality, from who I was, and all my insecurities.

I thought I had found the answer I was searching for. I believed that I had finally found the cure for what ailed me. I fell in love with Miss Marijuana because I fell in love with not being myself. I felt like I finally found a way to escape from the hidden insecurities that plagued my life.

I believed I had found the cure—the answer!

And do you know why that happened? As I look back on it I believe I felt like that because I really, truly, hated myself. You see, I didn't want to be me; and when I was high I took a journey outside of myself, I wasn't myself any longer.

With marijuana I finally became "The Hulk". In fact, I became The Hulk *and* Superman, all in one.

Under the influence of marijuana I was able to leap tall buildings in a single bound.

Look! It's a bird. No, it's a plane! No . . . It's Super Ronnnn!

At least that's how I felt for a while. I was still just Ronn after I landed on the runway of reality. And dealing with who I really was kept driving me quickly back. So I went back to marijuana again and again to take the next journey, the next trip, and find the next high.

All my insecurities disappeared when I entered fantasyland and became "Super Ronn." There was one problem though. The ticket provided only a brief visit. What I wanted was a one-way ticket to fantasyland, so every day I kept buying many tickets to that new found, amazing, marijuana wonderland.

But I was not alone on my journeys. Joan joined me in taking trips to fantasyland, and we both continued for a long time there in "the night of the mind."

Today it is a well-known fact that marijuana is a gateway drug. Don't let its legalization in many states fool you into thinking otherwise. It is indeed a gateway drug. It opens the door to many hellish addictions for many of its unsuspecting victims.

So don't let Miss Marijuana fool you. She is very cunning. She whispers in your ear:

"See, I told you I was harmless; so don't be afraid. There's no need to stop here; there are even better adventures out there for you to experience. Come; come with me, and I will introduce you to some of my cousins. They're harmless too."

Don't believe anything she says.

And for the ignorant and gullible marijuana opens the door for exploration—to coin a familiar phrase: "To boldly go where no man has gone before".

"Captain Irk".

"Yes Smock".

"What planet should we explore today?"

"Planet QUAA714 Captain Irk, from the distant Galaxy of "LUDE X".

Lude X contains many solar systems to explore, and they contain planets of pills and prescribed medications. There I found the planet system of Quaalude X. It was ruled by Queen Pill, commonly called Lude in street terms, or "714."

I thought Queen Lude was a godsend. She not only dissolved any and all my fears and insecurities but also increased my super powers from those of Super Ronn to those of Superstud.

And when I dissolved a 714 in wine . . . BAMM! Wherever I appeared with Lady Lude, Mr. Cool had just arrived. So I ditched Lady M—Miss Marijuana. She became a has been. And I became engaged to Lady Lude. I even started wearing a T-shirt with her special number and name on it: "Lude 714." She controlled me.

In a short time she not only ruled over the planets of the Quaalude X, she possessed me! I was hers, and she came to own me, mind, body, and soul.

> *Minds are never to be sold.* —William Cowper

Sad, but that is exactly what I did. I sold my mind. At this time in my life things really started to spiral out of control. Yet, I didn't even notice. Such is the treachery and deceptiveness of drugs. Clearly, ignorance results in deception. And for the next several years none of us ever saw any danger coming.

(To Joan's credit, I must make clear that she never used ludes. She was a rare bird. In fact she didn't move on to any other drugs even after many years of marijuana use. But her experience was rare among those of who live in an environment of drug use.)

Let me clarify an important truth here. There is a difference between a drug abuser who has a habit and a drug abuser who is addicted. A person with a habit still has a small hold on his or her "will" regarding drug use. Drug users with habits call their drug use recreational. But when people cross the line from habit to addiction, they no longer have a hold on their will. They think they do, but they do not. Their will is now controlled by the demon, the substance. Their mind has now been altered. All rationality has been swallowed up by the addiction.

I was now over my relationship with Miss Marijuana. Over her midnight munchies and the hysterical uncontrollable laughter that comes from hallucinating on the mind-altering drug. She was a fun date for a while. But I was no longer a novice. Now there was the great enhanced sex that came from an intimate relationship with Lady Lude that capped off the evening activities. Life was just one big party—or at least that's what we thought at the time.

Being the lady's man that I was in those days, I thought, "How could life get much better? I have it all!" I really felt like I had it all. No one could see the danger coming, especially me; for I was the first from my clique to officially move and take up permanent residence in Fantasyland, USA.

There is more stupidity around than hydrogen and it has longer shelf life. —Frank Zappa

I quickly became adept at processing drugs, a wannabe pharmacist if you will.

I actually carried around with me a Physician's Desk Reference (PDR) like a minister carries around a Bible, in order to know all the best "highs" in the world of pills.

I powdered the Quaaludes into a carafe of wine, and then I spread the joy around with a lady on each arm. It was party time— or so I thought—but there was many a time when I blacked out during the night and woke up the following morning behind a couch or on the floor, stark naked, with no remembrance of what had occurred that night.

I should have died many times from the combinations of drugs and alcohol that I consumed. There were actually times when I blacked out at an intersection after stopping at a traffic light only to regain consciousness the following morning—still sitting at the light with my foot on the brake and the engine badly overheating. I never moved from the spot. And shockingly enough, I was never even recognized or investigated by the police throughout those wee hours of the morning.

You see, we all thought that was funny. It was just something to laugh about, but in all reality it was just beginning. It was the *tip of the iceberg* of a deadly and dangerous path that I was entering. And it was a path that ultimately lead to the grave for many of my friends. (I use the term *friends* loosely—very loosely. More accurate terminology would be "street business associates.") Walking the same path nearly took my life numerous times.

By that time I was nearly twenty years old, and that means Joan was nearly eighteen. It was then that we decided to get married. *Getting married* was what young people did in the 1960s. People didn't *live together* like they do today. A good reputation meant something back then to most people—so in order for a young man to have the girl he wanted (in bed), he got married to her.

The wedding bells rang, and Joan and I got married. And it wasn't long before I fathered two sons with Joan over the course of a three-year time span (I had to prove my maleness). Two abortions then followed in the years ahead. I regret them now.

I may have fathered a third child with a beautiful neighbor during that time, but only DNA could verify that for certain. Even though I lived a double life while married, Joan and I were seen by most people in our circles of association as having what appeared to be a very happy marriage.

All during that time I never considered myself as having a drug problem. I worked as a union carpenter because of my experience as a young boy in working with my cousin Sal. He was an incredible handyman, and he could fix or build anything.

I certainly was a drug abuser, but I convinced myself that a drug abuser was not necessarily a drug addict. We were just having good clean fun, right? Rigggght.

Although I loved Joan (at least to the extent that back then I really knew what love was), I was as promiscuous as an alley cat in heat throughout our marriage. I actually kept a little black book that would put Bill Clinton's to shame.

I reserved Fridays for my wife—but Saturday through Thursday were reserved for Janet, Sue, Barbara, Tina, Gina, and Vickie, with a change of cast of characters every week.

Remember, the ludes transformed me into *Superstud*; no longer jumping over buildings in a single bound. Instead, I was able to leap from bedroom to bedroom in a single night.

I could literally be found walking out of our garden apartment's front door and into the back door of Joan's "best" friend's apartment—or the backdoor of our dynamite-looking, sexy babysitter in a neighboring apartment complex. I was living out all of my addictions.

After all those years, and after all my experiences in life, I was still on my search for acceptance. I continued to search for the comfort and security that I felt only my mother provided to me. And to me, my only chance of finding what satisfied my soul would be found in the arms of a woman, in the euphoria of a drug, or in both.

So I constantly searched for it through my relationships with one woman after another—one drug after another—one pill after another.

> *The danger in promiscuity is that it's always barking at your heels.* —Rick Springfield

People around me never knew it. They didn't see it, and they never could have understood it. But throughout all that period in my life I still remained insecure as a man. I still lacked confidence when it came to relating to all my male friends. All the time I was trying to prove my masculinity to women through my sexual prowess. Inwardly, I felt like a male reject, so my insecurities continued to drive me to both escape to fantasyland and seek out the arms of women where I was accepted.

I wasn't really simply seeking sexual gratification. It wasn't all about sex. I was looking for emotional security. I was searching for comfort, and my comfort zone, my only secure zone, had been in my mother's arms.

I needed what I felt my mother had provided to me as a young child. Inside I was still that little boy.

What many wise people have said in the past could not be any more true: your early years shape your life.

CHAPTER 5

THE AGE OF AQUARIUS

Marijuana being the gateway drug that it is has now led me to Quaaludes, which in turn has opened the door to a variety of prescription pills like Valium and Percocet, and many other popular pills during the 70's.

Pills became my drug of choice—my first love, as I wandered blindly down a very dangerous road of deception. I became so well educated with my PDR (*Physicians' Desk Reference*) that I would know all the actions, reactions, and side effects of every pill.

I was always looking for the pills that offered what I thought would bring me the best action. And after studying the PDR so diligently, I actually felt as if I could have donned a white coat and subbed for a pharmacist in any New York City pharmacy.

Of course, contrary to the warnings given by pharmacists, I always mixed in drinking a little wine with my pill-popping for some *special effects*.

A shot to kill the pain
A pill to drain the shame
A purge to stop the gain
A cut to break the vein
A smoke to ease the crave
A drink to win the game.
And addiction's an addiction,
Because because it all hurts the same.

—Michael Koon

To me, I was just having fun. I never saw the dangers lying ahead. I never wanted to. I was a stubborn, butt-headed Italian no one could reach or teach. I had all the answers. But although I was tough and stubborn on the outside, I was still that frightened little boy hidden inside. No one suspected the insecurities residing within me were tearing me apart. But they were driving me into deeper involvement with substances. It just all looked like… "Fun".

When I was twenty-three years old, the 3 Ps—Pot, Pills, and Promiscuity—defined my daily routine. I continued to work as a carpenter. I was still a good *unfaithful* husband to my wife, Joan. And I was a so-called father to two young, beautiful boys.

My sons never had a father spend one moment of quality time with them. I was either too busy in someone else's bed or getting high to escape my fears of reality. And even on the rare occasions when I was home, my mind was never really there.

No matter where this body is, the mind is free to go elsewhere.
—William H. Davies

I had no business being a father. My life, my experiences as a child, had not prepared me for the responsibility. I was completely ignorant of how to be a real dad, and I was absolutely clueless of the damage I was doing to their young lives and futures.

My sons were about three and four-years old when I made what I thought to be a harmless decision that ultimately changed my life and the lives of my family forever. I decided to accept an invitation to go to a New York Knicks scrimmage game at Monmouth College in Long Branch, in Jersey. I was still an avid gambler with the bookies and an avid Knicks fan, so I went on that fateful day to see them play.

While sitting in the bleachers at the game, I saw an angel. And Susan entered my life.

I heard the fanatical, screaming voice of a woman behind me shouting out something to one of the players. And as I turned around and looked up into the bleacher seats to see where the voice was coming from, there she was, making eye to eye contact with me.

We instantly locked onto one another with a steamy stare. There she was, a beautiful young woman with long, straight, brown hair down to her waist. She was petite and sexy, with a big responsive smile on her face. And again . . . I was hooked. I was instantly slain. I was powerless to resist her. My addictive nature took over.

My mind immediately left the Knicks game and honed in on her like a heat-seeking cruise missile programmed to conquer.

And being the well-accomplished flirt that I was, it didn't take long to score. Back then I had enough "lines" to put Bell Telephone out of business. And I was so shrewd and manipulative when it came to women that I think I could have written a New York Times Best Seller on how to score in one easy lesson.

I proceeded to penetrate her mind with unspoken words and motioned for her to come down, and she did. She came down to me like a child under a spell—like Dracula bidding his next victim who was powerless to resist. Need I say more?

For me, the Age of Aquarius had truly begun.

You see, Susan's "sign" was Aquarius. We were all into astrological signs back then—so much so that Susan and I both had our signs tattooed on our thighs. She had my sign tattooed on her, and I had her sign tattooed on me. (Memories still plague me every time I take a shower.)

My relationship with Susan was the beginning of yet another (actually the steepest and quickest) downhill turn in my life. And it was one that I should never have survived.

Keep in mind that I was still married to Joan at the time, but I was infatuated with Susan. She was wild, and I was willing. And at that time in my life there was nothing more I could want. We really bonded, and within two weeks I was living a double life. I lived half my time with my wife and half my time in a motel room with Susan, where we constantly enjoyed smoking pot, getting high on pills, and having sex.

Susan and I were *birds of a feather* when it came to drugs. As a matter of fact, it was not long after we met that I discovered she was more deeply involved than I was—much more. She had already graduated to harder drugs. She was already into cocaine, a lady to whom I had not yet been formally introduced.

Susan was just what I didn't need, but I was powerless to resist the temptation coming through that sexy woman. (I sympathize with you Samson.)

At that time she was dating a big-time cocaine dealer in Newark, who turned her on to cocaine. And the next thing I knew I was giving Susan $700 to buy an ounce of pure cocaine. She went alone to "cop" it because she was not sure how her dealer friend would receive me.

That is the day I made one of the biggest mistakes of my life. My graduation day arrived. I entered into the big time. Susan returned with the cocaine, and . . .

Bamm. BAMM! Helloooo.

CHAPTER 6

HEAVEROIN

It was all over. As that cocaine raced up my nose I felt like I had been launched off the pad as a rocket booster at Cape Kennedy. I blasted off and never looked back. There in orbit, traveling at 30,000 miles-per-hour, I discovered much more than the fantasyland I knew; I discovered another uncharted planet.

An intense love affair with Miss Cocaine instantly developed. Lady Lude and Miss Marijuana were now old relationships. I had another new love—Miss Cocaine.

With Miss Cocaine on my arm I was Super Ronn, Superstud, and Superstar all rolled into one.

Happiness lies within one's self, and the way to dig it out is cocaine.   —Aleister Crowley

Cocaine became the love of our lives. Dancing, bar hopping in New York City, cocaine, enhanced sex—I felt like I had the world on a string. I thought I had finally discovered my identity.

I finally knew who I was. I was THE MAN.

But I was the man behind the Mask. Yes! Thanks to Miss Cocaine I had been transformed into . . . into . . . into . . .

Remember the movie, The Mask, starring Jim Carrey as Stanley Ipkiss?. He found a mask with magical powers; and when he put it on, he found it brought to him powerful, extraordinary abilities. Remember what happened to Stanley whenever he put on the mask? Shy, timid, Stanley Ipkiss was transformed into his alter ego and became a maniac superhero.

Hellooo! That is what cocaine did to me. It changed me from a Stanley Ipkiss into a maniac superhero. Every time I put on the mask of cocaine I was instantly transformed from insecure to insane.

Invincible—irresistible—desirable...Superhero!!! I was "THE MAN" behind the MASK.

And as long as I was wearing *the mask*, there was nothing I wouldn't or couldn't do.

> *They shoulda called me Little Cocaine, I was sniffing so much of the stuff! My nose got big enough to back a diesel truck in, unload it, and drive it right out again.* —Little Richard

I soon met and became acquainted with Susan's dealer friend, Gene C. I will keep his last name confidential on the grounds that if he is still alive he more than likely would still come after me and kill me. In fact, he already tried once. He was a big-time dealer in Newark, and after meeting him I began doing business with him directly.

Gene was an ex-convict who was a violent unpredictable skitzo. We would ride over the Bridge Street Bridge that connects Newark and Harrison while he hung his .45 caliber snub nose out of the window to shoot out the bridge lights at night just for kicks.

He also possessed a monster cocaine habit, himself; and he often cooked up enough cocaine in a spoon and mainlined enough of it to stop a giant raptor dead in its tracks.

At that point in time, Susan and I *just* snorted cocaine. We were content with just flirting with the devil; we wanted nothing to do with sticking needles into our veins. However, it has been said that bad company corrupts good morals. And sure enough, we eventually found out that if you lie down with dogs often enough you will wake up with fleas.

And speaking of the dogs, let me introduce you to Charlie. He was one of Gene's shooting gallery buddies. (The shooting gallery is where addicts gather to shoot up.) We always found Charlie wasted on cocaine and heroin anytime we went to Newark to cop our drugs. And while there, he always badgered us to mainline, to shoot up, instead of snort.

He was always saying, "You are wasting it up your nose."

He badgered us time and time again. And one night I became so annoyed by it that I put my finger on his nose (literally) and said, "The day will never come that I will stick a needle in my arm."

I'll never forget that statement. But Charlie was persistent. He never gave up. He continually pushed and pushed and pushed us to shoot cocaine—and also heroin.

One fateful day he broke open a bag of heroin and said, "Here, snort this, it's on the house."

I hesitated because I thought only junkies did heroin, and I was no junkie! I was just an innocent guy having a good time. So I hesitated because of the stigma associated with heroin; but the curiosity I had about a heroin high became too much for me to handle.

Many inspirational speakers have said some variation of "Don't be afraid to go out on a limb. That's where the fruit is." Well, being tempted by the fruit I saw out on the end of the limb caused me to climb right out there.

Being the Italian butthead I referred to earlier, I convinced myself that, after all, it was "only snorting". I told myself, "what could a little snort do to me?"

The curiosity did the rest—temptation got the better of me, and I snorted the bag, the whole bag, the whole bag of pure heroin.

STUPID!

In her book, *Voices of the Faithful*, Beth Moore wrote:

Let's wise up. Some of us aren't fighting the fire, we're playing with fire; flirting with the devil. Stop it! Stop it now before all hell literally breaks loose.

Tooo Late!

All hell literally broke loose in my life.

While I still maintained a deep affection toward Lady Cocaine, it became time for me to move on in my education. I graduated again that day when I received my Master's Degree in Addiction. My thirst for *education* was becoming relentless. And it was actually on that very day when I started working on my *doctoral* thesis: *The Power of the King of Drugs.*

My attachment to Queen Lude was a thing of the past after King Heroin appeared to take the throne away from her and Lady Cocaine. King Heroin held great power, and I became his devoted subject.

King Heroin took his sword, laid it on my shoulder, and made me a knight in his realm. And as I lived under his rule I found myself becoming his love slave.

I instantly fell into the deepest love affair of all with a demon. A demon named heroin….

That demon, King Heroin, desired my soul; and he took it from me with little to no resistance on my part.

I had someone at the Houston police station shoot me with heroin so I could do a story about it. The experience was a special kind of hell. I came out understanding full well how one could be addicted to 'smack,' and quickly. —Dan Rather

To me, I had found *Heaveroin*. My body instantly became a mist. It had no substance. And I really thought that if I hadn't been carried down the stairway, I could have floated down it in a bubble.

He [the devil] can make men dance upon the brink of hell as though they were on the verge of heaven.
—Charles H. Spurgeon

Susan and I were dancing on the brink of hell. We were dancing with a demon.

Everything prior to our experience with heroin seemed like child's play. To us, taking heroin was the ultimate experience of life. I had climbed the ultimate ladder to success. "What more could there be to life?" I thought. I felt like there could be nothing more to attain.

I believed I had finally found peace with King Heroin. I had reached the pinnacle in my climb to the top; and there at the top I had struck pure gold. I no longer had a care in the world. All my insecurities were gone, finally—or were they?

> *It did not feel like something that was going to take over my life and destroy it. It felt like a subtle flower instead of a manipulative demon. That's the mystery of heroin.*
>
> —Corey Feldman

Susan and I began using both heroin and cocaine every day. Little by little it was consuming us, but we were completely ignorant of what was taking place. It was taking over our lives, but we never sensed the danger that was lying ahead for us.

We were completely unaware that we were becoming both physically and psychologically addicted; but we always wanted more and more. We never once thought we were out of control back then. We were just enjoying the euphoria the drugs brought to us.

Then, one night, Susan and I looked at each other dangerously.

Once again the demon's temptation and our own curiosity overruled our will.

"Let's do it. Let's shoot the dope. Let's mainline this heroin. Let's experience its full power and discover all its secrets."

I remembered the words that I had said to Charlie: "The day will never come that I will stick a needle in my arm." But that day came. It came once. Then it came again, and again, and again.

The rush of shooting heroin was instant, incomprehensible in effect, and irresistible. We shot up, and it was as if we became connected with King Heroin by a blood oath. Snorting dope was a thing of the past for us. That was a "waste of good smack." It was for the "novice," the children.

We moved into the big time.

Now if you are in the big time, you need to put in place a network of supply lines. An addict must have "connections" in order to be certain to always have what he or she craves. So I hooked up with a childhood "Boys Club" buddy, Larry, who I knew was an addict with local connections for heroin. And he turned me on to all of them.

CHAPTER 7

RISE AND DESCEND

I finally had it all. I had connections to the best high on the planet. I had a sexy and wild female companion, and I was driving an XKE Jaguar.

And from all outward appearances, people could imagine I was doing very well. To me, I was clearly the "MAN"—behind the Mask—just like in the movies.

> *Imagination is the only weapon in the war against reality.*
> —Lewis Carroll, Alice in Wonderland

Well, I had an imagination. In my mind I was *Ronn in Wonderland.*

As quoted earlier, it all felt like a subtle flower instead of a manipulative demon. That's the mystery of heroin.

Although Susan and I were clearly addicts, we still did not comprehend exactly what that meant. Did it mean like smoking cigarettes? No big thing.

After all, we were still functioning at our employments. It's not like we were incapacitated and living our lives leaned up against a wall in a filthy dark room.

But our world, our Fantasyland, suddenly began to quake one day when we had difficulty making connection with our dealers. This was the turning point.

We had run out of our supply of heroin for the first time. And although we simply felt apprehensive about it in the beginning—the way a person feels if he or she needs a cigarette—we suddenly began feeling queasy. We began wondering about the uneasy feeling we were experiencing. We wondered if we were coming down with the flu.

We then started to think we could have contracted some disease from using unclean needles. "What in the world is this? I've never felt like this before."

We had never known withdrawal symptoms before since we always had the dope on hand and regularly used it throughout each day. We also had no idea that a physical withdrawal begins to take place just hours after the absence of the opiate from the body.

We were ignorant that a physical addiction actually takes place. We were unaware of a physical and psychological addiction that would progress to become a living nightmare reality.

It was not long before I discovered that withdrawing addicts lost their composure in exactly the same manner that careless millionaires lose their money: gradually, then suddenly.

—Andrew Davidson

All of a sudden we felt a strange uneasiness, and then our muscles started to quiver and jump. Then we started to break out in sweats. And with the sweat came panic. Then we started losing control of our bowels.

We felt crazed. "What's happening?" we wondered. "What is happening to me!? What's happening to us?" Yes, all hell was breaking loose!

To go through heroin withdrawal is like having someone stick his arm down your throat, grab your stomach, and pull you inside out. Every cell in your body begins to light up, scream, and shake out of control. Your mind goes into an absolute state of panic that instructs you to do anything that it takes to get the cure—another bag of heroin! —Self

Susan and I learned fast, and we learned hard, what heroin withdrawal was. It was hell, pure hell—unlike anything anyone could ever imagine. Only an addict or an ex-addict can fully comprehend it.

We became frightened and desperate. And we knew that shooting dope wasn't a matter of choice anymore. King Heroin owned us, and he controlled our will. We then became bitter and angry.

"I thought you were my friend. I thought you solved all my problems. After all, you eliminated all my concerns and insecurities like you promised. Why are you turning on me now?"

We thought King Heroin loved us and cared for us! But we finally found him to be a consuming demon that only grows stronger and stronger as he torments the souls of gullible and ignorant people.

We finally got what we needed, and then we went about trying to secure more and better supply lines for heroin so we would never run out again. We thought better, more dependable contacts were the answer; but in making those connections we were actually digging the pit we were in deeper and deeper as our morals and values slowly dissolved.

And as our morals declined, our hopes and dreams for the future faded away. Fantasyland had been destroyed. The *fun* was over. Enjoying *the high* was over. Everything in our lives began revolving around the cycle of medicating ourselves throughout the day to get and stay "straight" so we could function. We became hardened.

> *The vine bears three kinds of grapes: the first of pleasure, the second of intoxication, the third of disgust.* —Diogenes

Our lives were reduced to "chasing the bag"—street lingo for daily pursuit of the best dope on the street. We first made connections in the Lower East Side of Manhattan. It was a hot bed for heroin at the time, with dealers openly promoting their products in broad daylight on the street corners.

We always knew where the best dope was because we could see where the crowds were gathering. The police drove through periodically, and that caused everyone to scatter; but within minutes the crowds would regroup like bees to their hive.

Anytime dope began to weaken, or be "cut" or mixed with other chemicals, where it lost its potency, we moved on to the next location where we heard the best product was being marketed. Harlem, Brooklyn, Bronx—we were chasing the bag everywhere. We were on *a mission.*

We learned the way of the streets quickly. And we began getting involved in things most people see only in the movies. But our actions were not being controlled by a script writer or movie director who could shout, "CUT!" We were actually living a real nightmare.

In the Williamsburg section of Brooklyn there were many abandoned buildings where the Latino gangs controlled the drug trade. There a person could enter a building through a large hole knocked through a block wall and discover hundreds of people from every walk of life waiting in line to cop their heroin.

City comptrollers, street sweeper drivers, and Wall Street executives all lined up with the junkies. There was no class distinction there. Everyone may have dressed differently, but everyone had one thing in common: they were all slaves to King Heroin.

Your "right of passage" to enter was show to one of the gang members the *tracks* on your arms from all your previous injections—no tracks, no entry. Once in, they lined up on a broken-down, two-story stairway with water leaking everywhere—no different than a scene you would see in a horror movie. This was one way they kept the undercover police from infiltrating the operation.

The gangs were very organized. They only carried a certain amount of heroin to each sale. Usually it was several hundred $10 bags. Once they had sold out, the gang members ran from rooftop to rooftop to deposit the money at their base. Then they brought back another supply to the waiting lines of buyers. That went on throughout the day or until the "Mother Load" ran out.

That was part of the underworld I spoke of in my introduction, where we maintained our invisibility. No one but those who lived in the underworld knew what was going on in those buildings. Children played down the street, while mothers walked their kids to school, never suspecting there was another world *right beneath their feet.*

It was not uncommon to see the police parked down the end of the block watching it all happen. They watched the people dipping in and out of the hell-hole in the wall. They knew what was happening, but they were no dummies. They wanted to go home to their families at night.

Those cops didn't want to tangle with gang members donning bandanas covering their faces and .357 magnums stuffed into their belts. Breaking up the drug markets was for the SWAT teams who would make raids from time to time. But writing a parking ticket or presenting a driver with a citation for speeding was all the action these cops were looking for.

That neighborhood was controlled by the Dominican gangs who had lookouts stationed on every corner. Only the addicts knew who they were. When we arrived to cop our drugs we always listened for one of two distinct calls that came from those lookouts as their voices echoed throughout the deserted streets of the "hood".

Before we entered the "hole". We listened for "Tato bien. Tato bien." That was Dominican street slang for "all clear, all good." But when they shouted "Bahondo! Bahondo!"—street for "Get down! Get down!"—everyone scattered like roaches under a spotlight.

I was waiting in line inside an abandoned building one day to cop my heroin, and suddenly I heard the call, "Bahondo! Bahondo!" Everyone dissolved into the woodwork in seconds. I ran frantically behind another man, and without thinking I followed him out of a doorway . . . to nowhere. But it was too late for me to stop, and I soon discovered that I was in mid-air, falling from the second floor.

"Hello, Hollywood? Need a stunt man?"

Surprisingly, I landed flat on my feet. (I have flat feet to this day.) I was badly stunned, and I had little to no feeling in my bruised legs and ankles. But incredibly, nothing was broken, so I somehow got up and continued running. (It's amazing what a little adrenaline can do for you—not to mention the fear of jail time.)

Hiding in the dark corners we waited for the all clear call, "Tato bien. Tato bien."

Everyone then returned to the lines knowing we may have to do it all over again at any moment.

That became my lifestyle—playing a cat-and-mouse game with the police every day. And little by little, day by day, month by month, heroin began to replace everything of value in our lives. All our finances and priorities in life began to disappear.

As for our families, we eventually alienated each of them, one by one, as we manipulated and stole from them to provide for our addiction. And after being fired from our jobs we began to completely withdraw from society.

My wife, Joan, tearfully filed for a long-overdue divorce. I was no longer able to live the double life, and I was not the same man she married. I could no longer hide the heroin addiction from her, and she eventually discovered I was running the streets for drugs with another woman.

In the beginning Joan furiously stalked Susan. She cut up her clothes and threatened her in an attempt to get out her out of our lives. But it was far too late. I was not in love with Susan. I was in love with heroin. And even though it turned on me, it owned me.

Susan and I then needed each other in new ways. We became deeply co-dependent. And that is common among addicts as they work together to support their habits.

It wasn't love that bonded us together, it was heroin that bonded us together.

Getting addicted to heroin is like getting married to the wrong woman; after a short honeymoon period, everything begins to systematically fall apart. —Anonymous

In order to support ourselves and our habits, Susan and I began dealing drugs. I bought large quantities from Gene in Newark, and we sold it locally for profit. Up until that time, Susan and I were still basically in Jersey, and we rented an apartment together in Asbury Park. We used that place as a base for our drug operations.

This continued for a while without any big problems. However, after returning to our apartment one day from one of our trips to Newark, we heard a knock on the door.

We opened the door, and there was Gene standing in the doorway—whom we had left only one hour earlier. He looked strange, and I sensed something was going down, so I slipped into the bedroom to hide the heroin and cocaine I had just purchased from him. As I turned to exit the bedroom, he was in my face with a .45 caliper snub nose pointed straight at me.

Now remember, this guy was looney. He was *bugged out!* Or in other words, he was suffering from *grand paranoia*—a common result of cocaine use. He was hallucinating big time and sweating profusely.

With the gun still held point-blank at my head, he gathered us into a corner claiming we had just robbed his drugs. With Gene was Rollo, his body guard—who also always carried a snub nosed .45 caliber pistol in his belt.

Gene told me to get the drugs. And I did. He grabbed the heroin and cocaine from my hands and then shoved us into the living room and onto the couch. Then, as Gene backed away from us toward the door (with his gun still pointed at us) he took aim and said to Rollo, "Should I kill them?"

It would have just been sport for that skitzo loon to do it, but Rollo, to whom we had actually become pretty close, said, "Nah, leave 'em alone."

Susan and I were in a state of shock as Gene continued to stare and stand there with his gun pointing at us while listening to Rollo's urging to go.

We both knew Gene was fully capable of pulling the trigger and thinking nothing of it. He hesitated for what seemed like an eternity, then he suddenly turned around and left.

Gene and Rollo fled the scene, but in the process they took not only the drugs we had purchased but also my Jag. And now we were not only without drugs, we were without a car.

> *Monsters exist, but they are too few in number to be truly dangerous. More dangerous are the common men, the functionaries ready to believe and to act without asking questions.* —Primo Levi

We couldn't speak. We were stunned. We were speechless for a good 30 minutes. But we were alive—barely.

With the drugs we bought to sell gone, and with our money that we had invested in our stock of drugs gone, we were forced to resort completely to stealing and manipulating in order to provide for our heroin addictions that were by that time spiraling out of control.

Withdrawals came more frequently—as close as three hours apart—making the demand for more and more heroin. And as we became more and more street hardened there was nothing we wouldn't do to get the fix that we so desperately needed.

For drug addicts, stealing from and manipulating their own families is usually where it begins. We became more and more immune to any moral convictions that held us back from stealing from anyone, or from doing anything we had to do to get what we needed to survive.

CHAPTER 8

THE GODFATHER

With an ever-deepening heroin addiction, no family, no job, and no money, what does a drug addict do? The answer is: whatever he must do to get a fix.

We needed money—big money. And we needed it fast. But believe it or not there were still a few final strings of moral fiber within me holding on for dear life. There were some activities associated with the hard-core drug arena that I still at that point refused to get involved in.

So I did what I felt like any respectable, ignorant, red–blooded Italian would do; I pursued connections I had with a New York/ New Jersey crime family. I made contact through the owner of a local fish and chips franchise (now deceased).

Thanks to the movie, *The Godfather* (which strongly influenced me) I believed that I finally found what I saw to be my true identity as a human being.

All my life, I've always wanted to be somebody, but I see now I should have been more specific.   —Lily Tomlin

I saw working for the mob as the way to give me a continuous source of big money that I could use to support our heroin addiction. However, before I could be interviewed by their representative I had to clean up my act.

That faction of the mob was strictly in the gambling business. They wanted nothing to do with drugs. And if they knew I was a drug abuser—much less a heroin addict with a girlfriend who also was a heroin addict—they would have never even considered me. It was a high stakes business, and that required someone who could run their office with excellence and loyalty, one who would never "rat" them out.

They had to have someone who could be completely trusted to keep the records of some of the highest betters on the east coast. They didn't want any part of a two-bit drug addict who could destroy their whole operation and get everyone sent to prison.

I was the person they were looking for. I came highly recommended from those within their circles. However, none of those who recommended me knew I had acquired a paralyzing heroin addiction. So I had to cover my tracks and appear to be the disciplined office manager they were looking for.

But how? How could I cover my paralyzing addiction and function normally?

The answer: methadone.

Methadone had just recently been introduced to the medical community to combat heroin addiction. It is an opiate blocker, but it's fully effective only at a high dose such as 90 to 120 mg. You see, I didn't want the 120 mg high dose of methadone. Thirty mg was a holding dose, and that will prevent a person from going into withdrawal without blocking out entirely a heroin high if you shoot a strong enough heroin dose. I wanted only 30 mg.

So shrewd Ronn made his way to a Manhattan drug clinic on 96th Street to "cry out for help." It was not easy getting on the new methadone programs back in the beginning since the so-called counselors were new and inexperienced in dealing with both the problem and the addicts. They had no compassion on those who came in sick from withdrawals. They made them sit and wait for hours before they could get a drink of methadone relief.

I vividly remember entering the 96th Street clinic nauseous, with my skin crawling and my bowels turning inside out, only to wait for three hours as they watched me suffer. That's the way it was in the early days of the methadone clinics.

But I knew I had to get accepted into the program if I wanted to be accepted by the mob. I thought the gambling operation was the answer to my problem. I was going to have all the money in the world to buy all the heroin in the world. That was my mindset.

My plan worked. I was accepted into the methadone program. Susan followed suit and also was accepted into the program. I had to report daily to the 96th Street location at 5:00 AM in order to get my "drink." I didn't have to worry about withdrawals for the time being unless I missed my drink. I could function. So I was ready to present myself to the "Family" coming with high recommendations.

As I already established, I was an avid gambler. I always thought it was in my Italian DNA. And I already knew all the bookies; so I put the word out that I was available for the position.

And voilà!—soon I was meeting with and being interviewed by local family bosses. They were interested in having someone they could trust work for them. He needed to be intelligent, but he also had to be willing to go to jail if he were to manage a major bookmaking operation with locations in Jersey and Staten Island. (For those of you who are wondering what "bookmaking" is, I'm not talking about manufacturing books.)

I fitted the mold, and I came highly recommended through a man named Richie.

Shortly after that, I was running the "offices" of an over three-million-dollar-a-week gambling ring in Staten Island, Manhattan, and Jersey—but not before some pretty intense testing and scrutinizing by the mob.

They tested me and checked my references, and they found out that I was "worthy" to go to jail for them if necessary. (Sucker!) As a matter of fact, they actually assured me that sooner or later I *would* go to jail for them. But I felt it was worth it, because I had finally become "somebody."

After all, bookmaking carried only a one to two year sentence. And I would be out in nine months on good behavior; so I was game. What did I have to lose? I had to support my drug habit, right?

Of course my drug habit was something that *la famiglia* could never know about. They wanted nothing to do with a drug-addicted bookie. So I hid my habit from them—something that was possible only if I had enough money to support my habit and continue reporting to my 5:00 a.m. daily appointment at the methadone clinic for medication.

Funded through my new position, I had the money to hide my addiction from them (at least for the time being), but it wasn't easy. Nevertheless, everything was cool, and I was back in the driver's seat—so I thought.

I was back in a position to bankroll our drug habits. And since *the family* also presented me with a rent-free apartment, Susan and I didn't need to worry about having a place to live. The apartment was on Third Avenue on the east side of Manhattan in a prestigious high-rise called The Wellesley. It was a classy place with a doorman and all.

I was also provided a nice classy Oldsmobile 98 Regency to drive. And with cash money in my pocket I could even purchase some cool paraphernalia for my drugs—among them, a gold spoon for my cocaine, scales, and Lidocaine to use for cutting the cocaine.

To me, I was *The Man* again! The mask was back on, and I was back in power. I had it all. I had a beautiful apartment, a great ride, money in my pocket, a sexy woman at my side, and all the heroin and cocaine I could dream of.

I was back in the driver's seat, and I no longer had to worry about any more withdrawals—or so I thought.

Now I believe I can hear the philosophers protesting that it can only be misery to live in folly, illusion, deception and ignorance, but it isn't -it's human. —Desiderius Erasmus

I operated the bookmaking office from *The Wellesley* seven days a week, every evening, and sometimes in the afternoons during baseball season. I closed the office to calls at 8:00 p.m. every night and took the elevator down to the lobby. The doorman always opened the doors for me with a big smile on his face, and I liked that. But I also thought it was funny. If he only knew he was catering to a low-life, heroin-addict bookie . . ..

I then jumped into my 98 Regency and bolted straight uptown to Harlem to cop a couple of "quarters" of heroin. I had the money—no more dime bags ($10 bags) for me.

I copped the dope, raced back to The Wellesley, and shot up all night long with Susan. What a life! We didn't think it could get any better than that.

Nothing in all the world is more dangerous than sincere ignorance and conscientious stupidity.

—Martin Luther King, Jr.

That continued for a number of years until Susan and I were discharged from the methadone program for failing to report every day, and for supplying urine samples that tested positive for the presence of heroin and cocaine. After that, we were no longer protected by the methadone blocker.

Once again we had to depend totally on our supply of street heroin to prevent withdrawals—and on the money from the bookmaking operation to purchase it. However, the more money an addict has, the more heroin he will use; and that just increases his ever-growing dependence. So it was getting harder and harder for me to hide my addiction from the bosses.

My body and mind were now craving a fix every one to two hours. And that was severely hindering my ability to take bets over the busy phones. It was hard to do business with a syringe in one hand and a phone in the other. Sometimes I was so "high" and incoherent while doing the books that I nodded off from near-overdoses. I was in deep, and getting desperate.

I was becoming less and less responsible at the office, and the bosses could see it. They no longer trusted me like they did in the beginning. I started receiving spontaneous, surprise visits from them to check on the office—and to check up on me.

They knew something was wrong. But the truth is, they needed me as much as I needed them. I needed their money, and they needed their fall-guy in case there was a bust. So they tolerated me. But I was playing with fire.

> *You heard of the double cross? In this business you gotta watch for the triple cross. You gotta always be alert. There's so much jealousy. Guys always trying to set you up, put you in traps. Trying to get ya killed. There was so much viciousness in this thing.*
> —Nick Caramandi

It was Super Bowl Sunday, January 25, 1987, and at 11:00 a.m. in the morning I returned to the office we temporarily rented on West 56th Street in Manhattan after picking up my fix on 127th in Harlem. That was five hours before the kickoff of one of the most highly publicized Super Bowls to date—Super Bowl XXI between the New York Giants and the Denver Broncos.

Turning on the television I could hear Pat Summerall and John Madden stirring up the viewers with their pre-game excitement. Kickoff was at 4:00 p.m., and I had to *open the phones* at noon to begin our bookmaking operation. But my body was starting to go into withdrawal with its telltale signs—runny nose, sweating, muscles jumping, twitching.

I had to get straight to be able to function before things started betting busy, so I quickly cooked up a hit of heroin and shot it. I got straight, opened the phones, and started taking bets. And bet they did. There was $5,000 on the Giants plus $8\frac{1}{2}$ points, $20,000 on the Giants plus $8\frac{1}{2}$, $50,000 on the Giants plus $8\frac{1}{2}$.

It was relentless, and I called our "man" in Vegas to check on the line. He screamed into the phone, "Lower the line! Lower the line!" I then lowered the line to 8, then to 7½ in an attempt to balance out the betting.

Then three o'clock rolled around, and withdrawal symptoms were setting in again. But this time I was out of control, and with the phones ringing off the hook, I panicked. Kickoff of the biggest game of the decade was only an hour away, and I was having a meltdown. Out of my mind and against every rule in the bookmakers' playbook, I took both phones off the hook to quickly cook and shoot up another hit of heroin to get straight.

I had to function or *la famiglia* would kill me!

I cooked up … I tied up … I shot up

I overdosed … .

Both phones were still off the hook, and our high rollers were going crazy trying to reach the office to place their bets before kickoff. They were panicking. And I was unconscious from a near-fatal dose of heroin.

For one full hour before kickoff our clientele was furiously reaching out to the bosses to find out what had happened, but the *Big Boys* couldn't risk coming to the office that day. It was far *too hot*. We were under observation by State Troopers from both New York and New Jersey. I was the fall guy.

I regained consciousness two hours later. The game was already underway. All betting had closed. The instant I realized what I had done I reached over and hung up the phones. Then they started ringing off the hook again, but this time it was not the clients who were calling; it was the big boys. And they exploded on me.

"What the %$#@$%! is going on with you? You %$$# $%@$# idiot!"

I was still disoriented and shaky, and I could hardly talk. I initially didn't understand what had happened.

Slowly I gathered my thoughts, and to save my neck I put the blame on a nonexistent Con Edison power outage in the building as the cause.

The betting was lopsided on the Giants who won 39–20, costing the bookmakers their single greatest loss in many years. They were furious.

> *I've seen many lives destroyed. I've seen more people have problems with gambling than I have with drugs and alcohol. And there are some serious consequences if you get in over your head.* —Michael Franzese

La famiglia was finally onto my drug addiction, and they wanted to kill me. But they needed me. They still needed their fall-guy, so they tolerated me for the time being. That said, in spite of the mistrust of the leaders, my association with the mob actually grew after that. I gained respect with some members of *the family* because of my ability to operate the office. As long as I was straight, I did good work.

Nevertheless, the heads of *la famiglia* still didn't trust me. I had broken their trust, and it was gone.

> *A mob is a group of persons with heads but no brains.*
>   —Thomas Fuller

Drawing on my experience and knowledge of *the street*, I finally came to think I could outsmart anyone and scheme my way through any kind of adventure that came my way.

I was caught up in the thrill of espionage and intrigued with *Miami Vice*, the popular T.V. series back then. I drew inspiration from it, and I was clearly over-confidant. Remember, I never took off my *mask*; I was always high on heroin and cocaine.

So, inspired by Miami Vice, I occasionally took time off from the bookmaking operation during the slower weeks of the sports season to take a few side-trips out of the country. I did that for a different faction of the mob to make some bigger money to support our addictions.

Ever the risk taker, I was no longer little timid Ronn. I was now a street-hardened drug addict making international drug runs.

One such run was to Panama, where I was to pick up cocaine from an unknown contact. I was to position myself in a certain, specific stall in a men's bathroom at the Panamanian Airport Hotel. I was to go there on a specific day, and at a specific time, and just wait.

I followed the instructions to the letter, and sure enough, right on time, I felt an attaché case being kicked under my feet from the stall next to me. I never saw the face of the man (or woman for that matter) who made the delivery, but the case was filled with pure cocaine.

Next I was to tape the cocaine to my body—about twenty to thirty kilos of the stuff—to my legs and around my waist.

But I didn't do that until I was in the cramped bathroom of a Boeing 747 at 30,000 feet on my return flight to JFK International in New York.

To pass through customs calmly without being flagged, Susan and I popped two 714 Quaaludes each to relax.

We were so mellowed out by the time we exited the plane that we literally floated out of the plane and right through customs together with wide silly grins on our faces. We were disguised as tourists, (camera, hat, tourists clothing, the whole nine yards); tourists who had just returned from a tour of the Panama Canal. Rigggggggggght.

There were no drug sniffing dogs at the airports in the 1980's like there are today. They would simply profile you.

I knew if we got busted I would go to jail for a very long time. (I'd likely still be in jail to this day.)

But who would profile two simple dumb looking tourists who just toured the Panama Canal?

It was an academy award performance.

How many know that once you "get over" you are emboldened and feel even more invincible? Well, I can tell you that is the way it is.

I felt like that trip was a successful audition for stardom. I was ready to take it to Hollywood. But of course, I wasn't playing a role in a movie. It was the real deal, with all the risks, and with no stunt men involved.

My next stop was London.

In London I was to meet up with a nameless man after several days in a prearranged hotel room. That man was, himself, returning to London from Thailand with the best heroin money could buy.

It was a potent opioid known as China White—highly sought after for its powerful effects.

U.S. Customs was harsh on anyone returning directly from Thailand, so the transfer was made in England. And with that arrangement, I once again cruised through customs—with pure heroin hidden in the bottom of shaving cream cans. The cans had been surgically cut, given a second, false-bottom that was installed near the top of the can, and filled with China White.

The shaving cream can even functioned. It had a little cream in the top with pressure on it. It worked like it should if a can were to be tested by customs. However, it was 3/4 filled with the precious white powder that was highly prized by the addicts and drug lords. It was so valuable, in fact, that I was actually devising an insane plan to rip off the mob. But they had a "welcoming committee" waiting for me at JFK International Airport when I returned.

I *got over* again. "Mr. Miami Vice"---yes sir---and ready for Hol-lay-wooood!!

> *Tricks and treachery are the practice of fools, that don't have brains enough to be honest.* —Benjamin Franklin

I made other side trips from my bookmaking activity to sell drugs to high class buyers in New York. Many of them were illicit gun dealers who displayed to me their attaché cases filled with the latest models of hand guns now operating on the streets.

As far as I was concerned I was on top of the world. The man with the mask had plenty of sex, drugs, and guns.

Groovin at high class clubs such as "Club Hippopotamus" on 61st Street and First Avenue in Manhattan.

What more could anyone want?

But my mind was so far from reality! My thinking was so flawed!

> *We are flawed creatures, all of us. Some of us think that means we should fix our flaws. But get rid of my flaws and there would be no one left.* —Sarah Vowell

CHAPTER 9

BUSTED

It was in 1977 when I began my bookmaking activities with a crime family, and Monmouth County, New Jersey had also launched one of its biggest all-out efforts—a joint effort with the New York State Police—to rid the Jersey Shore area of organized crime's gambling operations that had links with the big boys in Brooklyn.

All during that crackdown there was never a cessation of our gambling activities, just interruptions. We jumped from one office to another every week to stay one step ahead of the police raids.

It was a cat-and-mouse game as we moved around between Jersey, Staten Island, and Manhattan. We rented the apartments of friends and family for places to set up office for short periods of time. And we paid them handily.

We temporarily rented one particular, small, West Side Manhattan apartment on an upper floor from a girl named Donna (if I remember her name right). While there, she introduced me to Jerry—that's Jerry Seinfeld. (If you read this book, Jerry, you may remember our brief "hello".)

I assume he was dating Donna at the time, a waitress on Manhattan's west side. While he and her were "busy", I was in an adjoining kitchenette shooting heroin and doing book. Jerry hadn't made the big time yet, still doing stand up in the local comedy clubs and little known...So his name didn't impress me at the time.

Let me make it clear that Jerry Seinfeld was not involved in any way with the operation or with drugs. He was simply in the wrong apartment at the wrong time with the wrong girl.

The pressure was on at the time since we knew a statewide New Jersey bust was on the horizon. It was to reach all the way to Manhattan.

During one evening at the office—that is, at Donna's apartment—I heard shuffling outside in the hallway just as I was preparing to leave. I quickly gathered up all the gambling records for the evening and put them securely in my attaché case. Donna and her new boyfriend (not Jerry) were in another room in the apartment as I delicately moved toward the apartment door; and through the peek hole I thought I saw a figure flash across the doorway from one side to the other. But I wasn't quite sure.

I cautiously continued to look and wait. Then I slowly and quietly unlatched the door.

BANG! Instantly, New York and New Jersey State Police burst into the apartment. The door slammed me and threw me flying into the wall. I was stunned. The cocaine I had in my hand went flying, and papers went everywhere.

Surely you've seen on television or at the movies a portrayal of police raids bursting into a building and rounding up a bunch of criminals. Well, that's exactly how it all went down.

They placed everyone in the apartment under arrest, and that included Donna and her new boyfriend. We were taken to Central Booking in Manhattan. After grueling interrogation throughout the evening, the others were released the following morning, but not me. I was detained, threatened, and handcuffed to the bars of my jail cell in a painful position because I wouldn't tell the police what they wanted to know.

Now jail didn't scare me, but the withdrawal from heroin did. I knew it was just a matter of time before I was going to go into withdrawal if I couldn't get a hit. And before long I was beginning to panic because I knew the withdrawal would soon consume me if I didn't get released or bailed out fast.

By morning I was in full withdrawal. My skin was crawling; my muscles were on fire. Fortunately, the bosses sent a representative to my rescue that evening. I was in pain and sweating profusely when the jailer came to get me and take me before a judge. A mob lawyer arrived, and I was quickly released on bail. (Of course the big boys could never personally show their faces there.)

I was in panic mode after I was let out of jail, and I raced out and up to street level, where it was snowing and bitter cold against my sweating body. I ran right back to Donna's apartment, where I had been busted thirty-six hours earlier, and called Susan. Susan was in Jersey at the time, but she quickly returned to New York, met me with heroin and a syringe, and straightened me out.

Welcome to the world of the heroin addict.

But my release from jail wasn't the end of my trouble. I no sooner showed my face again there in New York, but sure enough, New Jersey State Police picked me up (in New York) and took me to Jersey.

New York was never the problem for me; it was Jersey. Bookmaking in New York rarely carried a prison or county jail sentence. Institutions in New York were too crowded, and they were too busy catching the *big fish* to be bothered with gambling issues. (And as a matter of fact, there were judges (now retired) who were some of our best customers.)

Within 48 hours I was busted again in New York and jailed in the Monmouth County Correctional Institution (MCCI) in Jersey.

No big problem. I was bailed out again by a mob lawyer; this time "before the ink dried", as one desk officer put it.

A Grand Jury was eventually formed after weeks of dealing with lawyers and court appearances. Our lawyers gave all of us who were busted strict instructions as to what we would answer if we were called to appear before the Grand Jury.

Basically, we were to say NOTHING.

We all took the Fifth… amendment that is. And take the Fifth I did. Even when I was asked my name, my response was, "I refuse to answer on the grounds that it may incriminate me." The prosecutors were hot and threatened us with indefinite jail time if we refused to cooperate.

Ensuing court matters followed us for the next 2 years until 1979 when finally, to protect my "fearless" leaders, I copped out to 2 years in the state prison to protect their identity.

They loved it. They had a fall guy who they could trust again.

And this new recognition gained me new respect in the mob while inflating my Italian ego to aspire to higher things.

Today a bookie. Tomorrow, the godfather!!! …..

Michael, Michael, Michael……….

Whenever I climb I am followed by a dog called 'Ego'.
                              —Friedrich Nietzsche

Throughout that period of time, during all the arrests and court appearances, I was continually struggling with a monkey on my back—a monster, my heroin addiction. But since I had so much money, I was able to sustain the habit and still function (if you want to call it *functioning*) for short periods of time.

I even had door-to-door drug delivery service. I had some taxi cab drivers getting drugs for me on the streets and delivering direct to my door. Cash is king as they say. Money buys anything.

But as fast as I received the cash, the heroin and cocaine consumed it. I could have $5,000 stuffed into my back pocket on a Friday night by my partner as we walked into the Victory Diner in Staten Island. Then over the weekend Susan and I would purchase and shoot so many *speedballs* (a mixture of heroin & cocaine) that by Monday morning I had no money to pay for the toll back over the Verrazano Bridge that linked Brooklyn to Staten Island.

The people manning the toll booth started turning me around and sending me back to Brooklyn after allowing me through several times. And I'm told they would say, "Here comes that crazy guy in that battered Mercury Marquis again."

I had blown the engine in the 98 Regency Oldsmobile the mob had provided for me. To allow them to collect on the insurance I was instructed to abandon the car on the corner of 67th Street and 11th Avenue on the west side of Manhattan. Shortly afterwards they sent "the boys" to pick up the car and crush it into a cube. It was then reported as a stolen car—never to be found again.

After two years of court postponements, the moment of truth finally arrived.

I was sentenced to prison and given thirty days to get prepared for turning myself in to be sent off to *Grandma's House* (otherwise known as the *big house*). Obviously I had never stopped using heroin; but I had already stopped using methadone that was protecting me from withdrawal. So my plan was to re-enter a thirty day methadone program so I could detox myself without suffering from withdrawal.

Then I purchased an ounce of pure heroin from a mob faction in Newark, cut it twenty times, and bagged hundreds of dime ($10) bags. The plan was for Susan to sell the bags while I was incarcerated in order to get money to sustain her addiction and meet our other financial needs. She also would have heroin to bring to me in prison on visits.

That was the second of three times that I was on methadone over a fifteen-year period. And I was a fool to think I could detox myself off heroin through methadone during the thirty days prior to entering prison. Just as I did the first time, I continued to abuse heroin even while on methadone over the thirty days prior to incarceration.

Instead of being detoxed upon entering into prison, I had a double habit. So my plan failed miserably (as my plans usually did), and as I once again entered MCCI, I entered with not only a paralyzing heroin addiction but also a methadone dependency.

I didn't comprehend what I was about to experience as I walked into that jail. There, I was going to meet up with the reality of my worst fears.

> *A wise man thinks ahead; a fool doesn't and even brags about it!* —Proverbs 13:16 TLB

Up until that point I was able to escape most severe withdrawal attacks simply because I had the finances and the substance. But those days were over. After I entered the institution, and they slammed that big steel door behind me, I no longer had control over anything. And I was not prepared for what was about to take place in my body.

On the morning of my entry into custody, I drank eighty milligrams of methadone and shot three bags of heroin as a last hurrah. To me at the time, that was to seal the suffering I was about to endure.

I was okay for about two days because of the methadone in my body. But on the third day my body began to fall apart; and for the next four days I had a *gorilla* on my back. I was delirious. Every muscle in my body was out of control. My stomach and my bowels were out of control—and my mind was out of control.

The wing of the jail I was in was greatly overcrowded, and there was *no room for me in the Inn,* so to speak. So they gave me a mattress and placed it on the floor by the urinals. And there I lay filthy and sweating for four days, kicking like a jackass, and completely out of my mind.

It was 1979, and there was no detox administered to those entering prison with addictions. They simply suffered. (There was not even a medical wing in MCCI in 1979.)

Some inmates tried to help me by giving me pills that I took by the mouthful. They went to the so-called *doctor*—an 85-year-old retiree—and requested sleeping meds for themselves so they could give them to me. By the grace of God I survived, but I was bitter and even more hardened. Who ever said incarceration rehabilitates?

In 1979 MCCI was recovering from prison riots, and the atmosphere was very tense. The conditions were harsh. The prisoners were kept caged up like animals, sometimes thirty to fifty men to a tier. And I received no moral support from the outside since I was forsaken by everyone I knew, including every one of my family members.

> *If you want to know who your friends are, get yourself a jail sentence.*
> —Charles Bukowski

CHAPTER 10

PASSING THROUGH THE WALL

My strength slowly returned. I was clean from drugs for the first time in many years, and I began to gain weight. I was drug-free, but of course I had no choice in that matter. After about forty days in the county jail I was transferred to Yardville, a youth detention facility used as a classification center for state prisoners being rerouted to their final destination.

After remaining in Yardville under lockup for about a month, I was finally transferred to minimum security at Trenton State Prison. But I didn't get to minimum security until I was classified at "the Wall"—as it was called—the high-security, main facility. The inmates held at the Wall were mostly lifers, and they would have had me for dinner if they could have gotten their hands on me.

The Wall was the old Trenton State Prison facility built before 1900 in an Egyptian architectural style. In short, it was little more than a dungeon. I'll never forget the first day I arrived there with another group of prisoners. Our hands and feet were shackled, and as I stood looking at the Wall in my fettered condition, I said to myself, "What the #*#@ am I doing here? This is crazy. I'm no murderer. I didn't kill anyone!"

As we dragged our chains through the prison corridors we were led past a darkened room where the old electric chair still stood. That little tour was compliments of the guard who wanted to put some fear in us new, green recruits.

And guess what? He did! Man, we were all filled with big-time butterflies. There are those who have said it's good to have butterflies in your stomach as long as you make them fly in formation. I couldn't get in touch with that sentiment at the time.

Then like we were a herd of cattle, the guards corralled us—about thirty of us—into one old small, archaic cell.

They closed us behind a manually operated gate using an old steel bar tool. I felt like I was in the Twilight Zone. This couldn't be happening.

I felt like I was in an old movie.

We were literally packed into the cell like sardines. We were in there sweating like pigs, and we couldn't move (no exaggeration) until the guards received clearance to move us into *population*.

Something I was not looking forward to—this was a mean prison.

But we couldn't breathe, literally, packed in like animals with many beginning to panic. Moving into population was a relief regardless of the dangerous predators who roamed the dark corridors in this hell hole.

Since we were on our way to the minimum security facility they put us into bright orange jump suits. We wore the orange clothes to distinguish us from the regular population when we walked to the mess hall to eat and then wait for transportation.

We stuck out like field mice in Central Park to a circling hawk.

> *The bird hunting a locust is unaware of the hawk hunting him*
> —Proverb

Then finally—FINALLY—we were bussed (still in shackles) to Trenton's minimum security facility. It was a work camp and a former State Police barracks.

But guess who knew I was coming? Guess who knew I was coming to dinner? It was all my *goombahs!*

I was met by a welcoming committee. To my surprise, the facility was *Little Italy.* All the missing bookmakers were there. All the white collar criminals were all there. And they were all waiting for me to join them.

We all stuck together and watched each other's back. They had their wives and families bring in the best of Italian home-cooked meals on their visitation days. Ha, I gained thirty pounds while there. I ate the best pasta and meatballs, eggplant, and even linguine with tuna Puttanesca! Would you believe! One would think I was eating at Angelo's on Mulberry Street in Little Italy during the Feast of San Gennaro.

Mangia, Mangia, Mangia, seven days a week. We even got our hands on a few cannolis. Ah, now that's an addiction that to this day I have yet to overcome.

> *Leave the gun. Take the cannolis.* —Clemenza

To be clear, not all of the convicts in the prison population were my goombahs. A majority, sure, but not all. There was also a small population of non-violent, small-time drug users and dealers. And it was through my association with that group that the demon heroin once again regained a stronghold in my life. A nearly fatal mistake. I was cruising along pretty well in doing my time in prison until I had the bright idea to bring in some of the heroin that I had left with Susan to deal while I was away.

The first thing I did was to have her smuggle in a syringe—the "spike" as it is known on the street. It was hidden in the bottom of what appeared to be a sealed cereal box. On the following visit, she brought in the heroin (pure uncut heroin).

She brought it to me in hollowed-out cigarettes with the packs resealed like they had never been opened.

I would lay the cigarette packs out in full view of the guards on the picnic table outside where we had our visits. I handled them like there was nothing to hide. It always worked.

I gave the guards no reason to be suspicious, and . . . well . . . the statute of limitations is up now, so, sorry guys. You win some, and you lose some.

Then I went into the prison yard with two other inmates (both of them heroin addicts). We went out like we were preparing to exercise. As we provided cover for each other I divided up the heroin (saving the greater portion for myself, of course), and we shot up.

I didn't consider that the tolerance I had built up from continuous use on the streets was gone. I knew the heroin was pure and powerful, but I thought I could handle it if I shot it low in my foot area. That way the effect would somewhat diminish by the time it traveled to my head. Or so I thought. I was so STUPID.

Well, shooting it into my foot didn't slow it down at all. It spread up my body and came on like a flash flood traveling through a mountain ravine. I reached out and clamped onto the arm of the inmate next to me like a vise. I looked at him square in the eyes, and said, "Help me; I'm going out. Don't leave me."

I knew I had made the fatal error, as so many before me. I was convinced I would die from this overdose.

The flood of heroin just kept coming. It wouldn't stop.

If I had gone unconscious (as I should have), the others would have scattered and left me there alone to die in the prison yard. They never would have incriminated themselves to save me. That was an understood law in the world of heroin. It would cost them additional years in prison, at "the Wall", not the minimum security facility they were presently in. It would have simply looked like one inmate went out in the yard and overdosed himself.

I would have done the same if it had been one of them. If you went over the edge with heroin, there was no one who really cared enough to pull you back.

911? Fagettaboutit...

The Edge... there is no honest way to explain it because the only people who really know where it is are the ones who have gone over. —Hunter S. Thompson

To everyone's amazement, I remained semi-conscious. But I was a zombie. It was like I was frozen. I couldn't talk or walk. They told me the pupils of my eyes were as small as a pinpoints.

I was "Dead Man Walking"; I should have died.

Looking back now, I realize it was nothing less than a miracle that I survived.

Since it looked like I was going to make it, the two inmates who were with me carried me back into the building. They didn't do it because they cared, though. They did it because they were afraid if they abandoned me in the yard I would rat them out to the guards who would have discovered me. They stood me up by my bunk like a wooden Indian at a cigar stand. And it was about time for inmate count.

All prisoners had to stand at their bunks for a headcount several times a day. During that headcount the other inmates literally held me up by leaning into me tightly on the left and on the right as the guard came by.

"Don't look at him in the eyes," they whispered to me over and over.

I was incoherent, but I didn't want to go to the Wall any more than they did. Somehow we made it through, and my overdose was never discovered.

> *Miracles happen everyday [sic], change your perception of what a miracle is and you'll see them all around you.*
> —Jon Bon Jovi

Nevertheless, I continued to have Susan bring in more heroin on a weekly basis. I worked as a mechanic in the prison garage, and I hid the heroin in the garage bathroom's shower stall. I hung the heroin on a string down into a hollow corner post. To gain access to the bathroom I would complain of severe stomach pain to give me enough time to shoot up. I didn't mainline, though; I "skin popped" an injection under the skin like a T.B. test. That provided a slow, gradual high that protected me against overdosing from the pure heroin.

One day I walked into the dorm area of the facility and noticed my goombahs were very somber and acting strange. They gathered around me, surrounded me, and braced me for some bad news from home. They were protecting me. They knew what they were about to tell me might cause me to flip out and run from the minimum security facility.

They informed me that Susan, whom I had married after Joan divorced me, had been seriously stabbed by an assailant. They told me she survived the stabbing but was in the hospital.

I lost control after hearing the details of the attack. I felt like a volcano preparing to explode. All I could think about was getting out of that place, finding the punk who did that to Susan, and making sure he felt what my wife had experienced. As far as I was concerned it had to be an eye for an eye.

I was crazy with vengeance. But my goombahs promised to help me take care of that dude after we all got out on the street again. They told me I had to settle down and wait for the perfect time.

The choices given to me were long range rifle or car bomb. They were serious, no joke—and so was I.

> *Before you embark on a journey of revenge, dig two graves.*
> —Confucius

Time passed, and Susan recovered. She was released from the hospital, and about four weeks after the attack she was strong enough to be driven to the prison to visit me.

The months slowly went by and I was "growing short" (jail lingo for *close to release date*). Finally, my parole hearing was scheduled before the parole board, and I was rehearsing for my academy award performance of My Rehabilitation. And sure enough, I played the role well, won my *Oscar*, and was scheduled to be released in two weeks.

Susan was still recovering from the knife wound when she came to pick me up on the day of my release.

In prison you must be jail wise and keep your cool, you must be an actor, internalizing everything, or at least as much as you can. However, on the day of my release, I exploded in the car.

All the emotions and frustrations that I had stored up but suppressed for months detonated. All the frustrations that I had held inside me while I was incarcerated came out at once, and I was out of control as I began pounding on the dashboard. I exploded.

> *When the prison doors open, the real dragon will fly out.*
> —Ho Chi Minh

But with the first taste of freedom, it was no longer revenge on my mind to kill this dude who stabbed my wife, but that demon who was wooing me back again, King Heroin. He was talking to me.

I obeyed. I went immediately back to him within the very first hour of my release from the prison, going directly from the prison to the street to be reconciled again to this strange love/hate affair with heroin.

But why? Why? What is this hold heroin has on me?

Dear Heroin
I never want to touch you ever again, you've ruined my life, made me steal from my family, on probation 'cause of you, why I choose you I don't know.

—Hannah Meredith

CHAPTER 11

TRAPPED

Susan and I remained in Jersey after my release from prison. We really had no choice since I was paroled to New Jersey. I was being monitored by the New Jersey State Police Organized Crime Unit, and I was *too hot* of a crime figure to go back to my bookmaking activities. So it was easy for me to quickly fall back into my old patterns of drug abuse. But this time I was going even deeper into a depraved, addictive state.

It wasn't long before Susan and I were living in one dive motel after another, dealing street drugs from the Montego Bay Motel on Kingsley Street in Asbury Park as blown out junkies quickly wasting away.

Trapped by our severe addictions, all sense of any remaining decency that we struggled to hold on to quickly disappeared. Susan and I fell fast, and we lost all moral restraint. More than before, our lives revolved around no more than doing drugs.

The world for us was about nothing but surviving. And it was dog eat dog. If we weren't street smart and willing to do anything we had to do in order to survive, regardless of the activity and the consequences, we knew we would not survive much longer.

By that time I was suffering from heroin withdrawals every two hours without a fix, and I was incapacitated most of the time. Susan began to sell her body through an "escort" service as most female junkies do when they find themselves in a desperate hopeless situation like ours. That is the way we got the drugs we needed every day. And even then it became a struggle to survive on a daily basis. We were trapped with no money, no car, and— with our paralyzing addictions—no hope.

Then a very strange thing happened. Susan, in the midst of her addiction, had an overwhelming desire to have a baby.

At the stage of addiction we were in, a drug addict has no desire for sex, much less care about having a child. But for two months Susan could not escape the overwhelming desire to have a baby.

I wanted nothing to do with sex, but she was persistent. And in the midst of our depraved existence, Susan became pregnant and gave birth to my daughter, Tiffani, in 1983. For the entire nine months of her pregnancy, Susan not only stopped smoking cigarettes but also detoxed herself from heroin and remained drug free.

It was amazing. If you ever doubted miracles, surely this should make you a believer.

However, that was not the case with me. After all, I was not pregnant. I continued hopelessly in my addiction to heroin throughout Susan's pregnancy. But interestingly, when little Tiffani was born, a certain desire and power to escape our self-made prison came upon me.

I went for help to a clinic once again and signed up on a methadone maintenance program, which enabled me to begin to function to some degree.

And guess who I called upon for assistance? No, I didn't ask God for divine intervention. I once again turned to the mob. I informed them that I was straight and ready to get back into action.

So taking methadone to maintain my sanity, I cleaned myself up and met with the bosses. And believe it or not I actually convinced them I was straight enough to run another booking office. I had skills and experience that were still valuable to them, so soon after our meeting they set us up in an apartment in Staten Island with our new baby and put me back on the phones. I was back in business—at least temporarily.

Although Susan and I both were on a daily methadone program at Staten Island University Hospital, it wasn't long before we again fell prey to the voice of heroin calling us. While still on the program our addiction took off again at cheetah speed.

If you think things were crazy for us before, get ready for insanity. While once again running a three-million-dollar-a-week bookmaking ring in Staten Island, we began to fall apart.

We were once again back to *square one*. We were using the methadone program to cover up our heroin and cocaine dependencies. The methadone enabled me to at least function in the bookmaking office since it prevented withdrawals.

Keep in mind that we had a little baby, my daughter, Tiffani, to care for. Yet we spent every penny we had on heroin and found ourselves unable to buy diapers and formula for little Tiffani or pay the utility bills. I used all the money given to me by the mob for our rent and utilities to buy heroin. I was once again digging a deep, dangerous hole.

The darkest years of our lives—the years during which our loss of moral restraint displayed itself most vividly—were from 1981 to 1987. My father died in July of 1982 while living in Florida, and my mother died in April 1985 at the height of my deepest addiction.

I wasn't able to attend either of their funerals. I did not want to be exposed to any family members. I was a hopeless junkie, and they all knew it. And did I spend any time in mourning over any of it? Nah. The only thing an addict mourns over is bad heroin. Desensitized by the drug itself, and constantly preoccupied with the need to survive, death to an addict is nothing more than an alternative state of life.

Dehumanized and functioning with altered minds, we would do anything necessary to get the heroin needed to sustain us. We craved heroin more than life itself, and our warped minds and bodies demanded it to survive no less than the oxygen we needed to breathe. We were experiencing pure insanity as we became totally withdrawn from any social contact with the outside world.

> *How strange to have failed as a social creature—even criminals do not fail that way—they are the law's "Loyal Opposition," so to speak. But the insane are always mere guests on earth, eternal strangers carrying around broken decalogues that they cannot read.*   —F. Scott Fitzgerald

Susan and I even began to turn on each other. I began to sell my daily methadone bottles on the street for extra money to buy heroin without telling her. But it wasn't long before I was discharged from the methadone program after being tested positive for opiates.

There was no longer any semblance of affection in our relationship. Our bond became purely a drug "connection," not a soul link. But we remained codependent. We stuck together because we needed each other to manipulate the streets and anyone who came within three feet of us.

There never was any genuine relationship between us. It was born on sex and drugs and it later died the same way.

The cocaine we were using made us both paranoid. We began to distrust each other. We found ourselves sleeping with the enemy, so to speak. The only loyalty left was to King Heroin. He continued his harsh rule over our lives. Self-preservation ends up being the only thing that moves the mind of a heroin addict. There was no love or concern left within us for anyone.

There finally came a time when I became excess baggage to Susan. I could no longer find favor with even the mob. I could no longer be a street asset or produce my share of money for our drugs. Susan needed heroin, so she ran off with a drug dealer who would provide to her what she needed. I was furious, but not because she left me, because she ran off with my daughter— dragging one-year-old Tiffani around from dope house to dope house in Red Hook, Brooklyn.

I lost my mind (that is, what was left of it). I didn't know where my daughter was, and I knew she could be sexually molested or easily kidnapped. As insane as I was, it was always my little daughter Tiffani who had the power to bring an occasional, brief period of sanity back into my life.

> *I became insane, with long intervals of horrible sanity.*
> —Edgar Allan Poe

There is something about the love of a father for a daughter where even heroin loses some of its power.

Since Susan was dependent on methadone, I knew she had to report to Richmond Memorial Hospital every day for her dosage. So I staked out the grounds until I spotted her entering the hospital with her dealer-friend. As I walked up to confront him he quickly turned and sucker-punched me. I was stunned, and then I went after him. We wrestled on the lobby floor as other people in the hospital became spectators until a security guard stopped the fight and separated us.

I confronted him and Susan again outside the hospital, but this time I was jumped by several of his friends. They slammed me to the ground, put a gun to my temple, and warned me to stay away from Susan and Tiffani.

> *Never underestimate the power of human stupidity.*
> —Robert A. Heinlein

Since I was no Mohammed Ali, I wisely retreated. Imagine that, I still a few brain cells left. But I continued to pursue my daughter and hoped to find a way to take her back. They hid her away and began following me even as I was following them. It became a cat-and-mouse game.

On one occasion I spotted Susan and her new boyfriend in the Savon parking lot on Staten Island, but I couldn't see my daughter. I ran from car to car, ducking from their sight, as I tried to see if Tiffani was with them. But it was to no avail. They suddenly disappeared.

I searched for them every day. I went back to the methadone clinic day after day knowing she had to show up sometime. But she never again did.

I began to ask around the clinic if anyone knew where they had disappeared to. Finally, through one informant, I was told they had gone to Florida, to the Fort Lauderdale area. Because of her need for methadone, I knew all I had to do was check all the methadone clinics in the Fort Lauderdale area to find her.

My daughter was taken from me. And if you've seen the movie Taken, I assure you that I had no less a passion to pursue and find my daughter than Bryan Mills (played by Liam Neeson) in the movie as he tracked down his kidnapped daughter.

Unfortunately, unlike Mills, I was no retired government operative. But even with my paralyzing heroin addiction, I continued after them with vengeance. I had no CIA training, but I was street wise, and I was able to track her down to a specific clinic in Fort Lauderdale.

I manipulated my informant, who had a car, and convinced him to take me to Florida. We took off and raced down to Fort Lauderdale in hopes of getting my daughter back. And I also hoped to repay a debt by beating the %#@%* out of Susan's dealer-friend with a baseball bat.

Thirty hours later we arrived and located the clinic, but we couldn't spot them. Then after several days of searching in the hot Florida sun, we lost their trail and returned to New York.

Weeks went by, and then suddenly I received a call from Susan. She told me she had had enough of her dealer boyfriend and asked if I would help her escape from him. She informed me they were about to return back to New York. I would do anything to get my daughter back, so I agreed to help her.

Susan and I devised a plan for her to lure him through a Jersey Shore town on the way back by saying she had to stop at my sister's house in Belmar. I was waiting at a pre-selected location with a Hank Aaron baseball bat, and the bat had her dealer's name written all over it.

After they stopped at my sister's house, I followed them in a car to Main Street in Bradley Beach. It was about two o'clock in the morning. At the right time I floored the accelerator, raced in front of them, and cut him off, pushing him to the curb (just like in the movies).

I jumped out of my car, and before he knew what was happening I raced to the side of his car like a crazy man with my Hank Aaron bat, screaming, "Out of the car, all of you!"

I forced Susan (of course she was in on it) into my car with Tiffani, my daughter, and I threatened him not to move an inch or follow me, or I would send his head over the right field fence. Believe me, he was scared stiff.

I had my daughter back, and she had not been harmed. As for Susan's dealer-friend, we never saw that guy again.

I wish I could say from that point on we all lived happily ever after. But that would be wishful thinking. We simply picked up from where we left off in Staten Island, racing back and forth to Brooklyn, chasing the bag.

CHAPTER 12

PUTTING ON THE BRAKES

No license. No registration. No insurance. And NO BRAKES! (And no brains.) That's right; I had no brakes. I was racing all over the boroughs of New York with no brakes—only an emergency brake—in a huge beat up Mercury Marquis.

I barreled down the streets of Staten Island and Brooklyn bumping into the back of one car after another like it was a demolition derby. I always attempted to stop by using the emergency brake; but with the combination of depending solely on the emergency brake and being high on heroin, I often calculated my stopping distance wrong. I slammed into the back of cars every day, then raced off.

A person could get away with that in New York. Ha, I love New York.

When I drove that car down the street it was like something you would see in a Three Stooges movie. I was a one man wrecking crew.

One day, out of control as usual—and freaking out because I was sick from withdrawals and getting sicker by the minute—I was having trouble finding my primary heroin dealer for my fix. I got word that there was some good smack over in the Cadman Plaza area, in a park located on the border between the Brooklyn Heights historic neighborhood and Downtown Brooklyn.

So Susan and I jumped into my beast of a car, a 1979, 4,000 pound (3,983 lbs. to be exact) Mercury Marquis, and took off. We called it "The Tank." Keep in mind there were no brakes, and by that time even the emergency brake was nearly burned out.

We swerved onto the BQE (Brooklyn-Queens Expressway) and headed north to the Cadman Plaza exit where the dealer was known to be at a specified location. That was one scene I am certain Hollywood would have loved to film.

Anyone who is familiar with the BQE will know that just north of the Atlantic Avenue exit there are two exits before Cadman Plaza. One is for the Manhattan Bridge, and the other is for the Brooklyn Bridge. And those exits arrive quickly as people drive clockwise around a blind—and I do mean blind—bend.

Well now, I guess you can imagine what happened next as I barreled down the freeway. No, no, you probably could never believe it. Fasten your seat belts.

I came around the blind bend doing 85 mph, just like Jason Bourne in the tunnel scene in the movie, *The Bourne Identity*. As I came around the bend I saw a wall of cars in front of me all backed up, trying to get onto the exit ramps for both bridges.

Cars were converging from both outside and inside lanes, standing still, and blocking the roadway.

So where does that leave me? Think fast.

Looking for a middle lane on a two lane highway. Helloooo... And here I came at 85 mph with no daylight between cars. NO BRAKES, and again ....NO BRAINS.

> *There are three different kinds of brains, the one understands things unassisted, the other understands things when shown by others, and the third understands neither alone nor with the explanations of others. The first kind is most excellent, the second kind also excellent, but the third useless.*
> —Niccolò Machiavelli

Let's see, considering what Niccolò said, above, it seems pretty obvious that I was operating on . . . hmmm . . . brain type three.

To be honest, there was a little daylight in front of me as I approached the traffic jam. I'd say it was two-feet wide, about enough room for a small motorcycle to get through. The problem, of course, was that my beat-up wreck of a Mercury Marquis was as wide as the Queen Mary. OK, that's an exaggeration. According to specs its outside width was 6.4583 feet.

I was never too good at math or algebra, but my little brain computed that a 6 ½ foot-wide vehicle cannot fit through a two foot opening; 6 ½ goes into 2—BAM!—that's right! So I had a choice to make, and I had to choose quickly. It was either the two-foot-wide opening or the Hudson River for us. And since I cannot stand polluted water, and wasn't ready for a bath, I went for the daylight.

My mind zeroed in on the target space with laser accuracy. And like the alien in "Terminator" I took aim…. and BANG!!!

Blasting through the small space between two cars, I sent them careering to each side like they were toys. It was just like a scene on Tru TV's Most Crazy Car Chases. Jason Bourne would be so proud of me. I could have been a star.

In a state of panic (well, wouldn't you have been?), I raced on furiously, speeding up to over 90 mph to escape the carnage and, of course, any police or angry motorists who might attempt to chase after me.

If I had been in Jersey, I would not have had a chance. I would have had more police cars chasing me than O.J. Simpson on the day of his arrest. But we were in New York, and I knew how and where to run and hide—and hide fast. So that was my plan.

Did I say hide? I looked over my right shoulder, and suddenly, to my amazement I was being chased by one of the cars that I blasted away. I couldn't believe it. His front bumper was sticking straight out like a swordfish.

Allow me to pause for a moment to assure you that what I am telling you is not an exaggeration. It has been said that truth is stranger than fiction.

The man in that car was furiously waving his fist for me to stop. And all the while, I was motioning back to him and mouthing to him that I couldn't stop. Read my lips!

"IIIII . . . CANN . . . NOTT . . . STOPP! NOOO . . . BRAKES!"

Can you picture that? It would have been an award winning scene for America's Funniest Home Videos if it had been caught on camera. But it wasn't funny at the time. I thought the guy was going to kill me.

Miraculously, no one was hurt during the experience. An even greater miracle to me, though, was that no cops ever came. Ha, again! Oh, how I love New York.

I eventually came to a stop, played dumb and apologetic, and calmed the man down with a sob story. It was another Academy Award winning performance for me.

Manipulating people is an addict's primary survival skill, but he obviously was not a New Yorker.

I gave him my worthless and expired insurance information with a phony name and address (I went by the name of Richie). And he went on his way after we pushed his sword—I mean bumper—somewhat back into place. I promised him that I would be in touch with him and send him a check (Rigggggght).

Don't hold your breath, Jack. I knew then without a doubt he definitely was not a New Yorker. Probably from Mayberry USA.

Anyway, I had to work out that matter fast and get back on the road. I had to get out of there before the police showed up and before my heroin dealer sold out.

There was no serious damage to *The Tank*, so I got back in the car and raced on to my original destination to pick up my dope. Withdrawal symptoms were beginning to set in right on time.

I previously mentioned that the police didn't show up. But prior to that there were times when they did. In prior auto incidents when I had encounters with the police, they just wrote out tickets to me and bolted.

Many New York City policemen don't like spending time with annoying paperwork on insignificant traffic matters. They have bigger fish to fry. Taking me down to the station would mean they would get home late for dinner. And then later they would have to spend time in court.

I called the tickets they wrote out and handed to me, "wish tickets." I took them, added them to my collection, hopped back into the car, and continued to drive like always until the next traffic stop. Then the cycle was simply repeated.

Actually, I was pretty good driving with the emergency brake most of the time. But here's a warning for you: don't try to duplicate that kind of driving unless you are a professional drug addict with a #3 brain type.

Heroin addiction is like driving a car with the steering going out. You eventually resign yourself to the inevitability of what's going to happen. —David Bowie

Through another of my traffic experiences (just one of many), I learned that there absolutely has to be angels nearby.

Susan and I were in the car, racing along from Staten Island to Brooklyn at 5:30 in the morning to cop heroin (as usual). And I was sick from my daily withdrawal (also, as usual). My son, Ron, who was staying with us at the time, was in the car with us along with little Tiffani and her rabbit, Bugs. (Don't ask.)

While again speeding wildly at 85 mph down the BQE, (that was my average speed) I actually blacked out from withdrawal and exhaustion. The BQE back in the early '80s was listed as one of the ten most notorious highways in America. There was always a string of abandoned and stripped vehicles on the narrow shoulders all along the way (but not so today).

Unbeknownst to me, there was an abandoned, stripped car sitting in the middle of the left, high-speed lane of the two lane roadway. Dead, sitting there. And here I come, 85 mph, unconscious at the wheel in that very lane with everyone sleeping.

Suddenly, the car shook violently like a train shakes when two trains pass each other on the tracks at high speed. I was jolted awake with a loud, *whoosh!*

Our car had delicately drifted over into the right lane at the last second while I was blacked out. And we must have come within a millimeter of the abandoned vehicle. Passing so close at that speed created a vacuum of air that nearly spun me out of control.

I jumped up, shaken and disorientated for at least 60 seconds, and tried to gather my thoughts about what had just happened. I looked in the rearview mirror and saw the other vehicle sitting in the middle of the road behind us.

I knew I was completely *out*, and if our car hadn't "drifted" over at the last moment we would have plowed into that abandoned car, and we would have been flattened like mosquitoes on a windshield. We would have never known what hit us. We would have become just another statistic published by the New York *Daily News.*

Do you believe in miracles, yet? I do.

> *I think miracles exist in part as gifts and in part as clues that there is something beyond the flat world we see.*
> —Peggy Noonan

Regarding my son, Ron, who was with us, he was eighteen at the time and had sought me out in Staten Island. He knew what was going on in my life, and he was afraid he was going to lose his dad to an overdose. He wanted to help me, and his solution was to come and live with me.

His plan was to keep me alive, but I also developed plans for him. A heroin addict becomes a master manipulator who will use anyone and anything to achieve his goal. And anyone includes his children.

> *The basic tool for the manipulation of reality is the manipulation of words. If you can control the meaning of words, you can control the people who must use the words.* —Philip K. Dick

My own son became a victim living within my realm of influence, and I seized the opportunity to use and control my own son to my benefit. I began by forcing him to rob and steal to support my habit. He was young, and I was able to manipulate him by playing on his emotions. I used his feelings of loyalty toward me.

But it wasn't long before he began to grow into the character of his father, and he, too, began to abuse drugs himself.

> *The greatest penalty of evildoing—namely, to grow into the likeness of bad men.* —Plato

CHAPTER 13

DEAD MAN WALKING

Although no longer bookmaking, we were holding on to an apartment in Staten Island (just barely) rented and paid for by the bosses. I could barely function, and they were afraid of allowing me to continue.

I couldn't hide my erratic behavior any longer and they suspected I was skimming thousands of dollars from them. And they were right, I was—to supply the never ending hunger of heroin addiction. They suspected it, but they couldn't prove it...

Every penny we had went to the drugs. The utilities in the apartment eventually were turned off, so we lived by kerosene lamps, oatmeal, and dirty diapers, unless I could score shoplifting at nearby Savon.

I became so desperate and crazy that I busted through a wall in our apartment and tapped into the upstairs tenant's electric line using auto jumper cables. (What was I thinking?) That worked for a while until I almost electrocuted myself by shorting out a neighborhood transformer on an outside pole.

BOOOOM! Happy New Year!

If there was even an inkling of any rational thinking that might have still existed in me, you would never have known it. Heroin and cocaine, the hellish twins, completely controlled our altered minds. Nothing else mattered. Food, sex, personal hygiene—nothing mattered.

> *I had not taken a bath in a year nor changed my clothes or removed them except to stick a needle every hour in the fibrous grey wooden flesh of heroin addiction. . . . I did absolutely nothing.* —William S. Burroughs

We continued to misuse all rent money the mob was still giving to us, so we were not surprised when, after several months of that, the apartment owners padlocked our doors.

Susan and I, with Tiffani, went to Brooklyn and left everything behind. Every personal thing we owned in the world was gone then. We had nothing but the clothes on our backs. In one of my rare moments of semi-sanity and sincerity, I sent my son back to Jersey and would not let him come with us to Brooklyn.

We returned once again to the Red Hook section of Brooklyn to be closer to the king, King Heroin. But this time we would remain.

We soon blended into the dangerous drug culture of Red Hook, but now with a very young child.

Even in my demented condition I was doing everything I could to hold onto my little daughter. She was the only positive thing in my life that still made me feel like a human being. She was the only reason I was still holding onto my worthless life. But realizing the great danger to her safety in Red Hook, I could see that keeping Tiffani with me for my benefit was being selfish.

I knew I was slipping away. I knew there was no way out for me and no longer any hope that I was going to make it. King Heroin had drained the last bit of hope from us. So I agreed with Susan to let go of my life preserver—my baby, my love, my little girl—my Tiffani.

According to legend, when an elephant senses its death is imminent it instinctively goes to an elephant's graveyard. It then dies there alone, far from the group—far from its family.Red Hook was going to be our graveyard.

We returned there because we believed death was imminent. Our minds were severely affected, clouded—convinced this is where the last chapter of our worthless lives would end.

So I let go of my little girl. I knew I was unable to protect her any longer so I called on my sister in Jersey to come and get Tiffani.

The image remains vivid in my mind to this day, the day I had to give my baby doll away to my sister. I was falling apart fast. I had no choice.

The transaction took place close to the expressway, just off the BQE Hamilton Avenue exit. I didn't want my sister to see how I was living or risk her safety by allowing her to enter into a dangerous environment where bullets frequently flew. So I met her at the expressway edge, away from the *projects*.

I waved goodbye to my little baby girl not knowing if I would ever see her again.

The moment I turned Tiffani over to my sister, I died inside. After that, I assure you, life meant absolutely nothing to me. The daily struggle for Susan and me to survive had taken its toll. It didn't matter to us any longer whether we lived or died.

Hopelessness is a terrible thing. The deceptive demon that lives in heroin had its way with us. And we could hear him laughing as he enjoyed the spectacle before him.

Hopelessness is like the vacuum of space—empty, cold,
* dark, alone.*
Hopelessness is isolation from the human race.
Hopelessness is the absence of life.
Hopelessness is heroin's promise.

—Self

That was at the end of 1984, and for the next two years, 1985 and 1986, I was simply a *dead man walking*—as was Susan.

Someone may ask how we could have slipped so far away from reality. But that was reality for us—a living nightmare we were hoping to wake up from. We were the living dead.

Like a condemned prisoner walking from his prison cell to his place of execution, a drug addict is a *dead man walking*.

The jailer calls out, "Dead Man Walking". King Heroin calls out in the same fashion to his victims, "Dead Man Walking".

Why would we want to live any longer in such a depraved state?.

> *I didn't really want to live, so anything that was an investment in time made me angry . . . but also I just felt sad. When the hopelessness is hurting you, it's the fixtures and fittings that finish you off.*
> —Angelina Jolie

Two NFL players gave up hope in 2009 off the coast of Florida, in the Gulf of Mexico, after a sudden, violent storm capsized their boat. There were four men in the boat enjoying a fishing expedition. The lone survivor of the accident told their story.

After the boat capsized they all—wearing life vests—clung to their overturned vessel for two to four hours. Then, becoming weary and suffering in the frigid water, one of the NFL players removed his life jacket and let himself be swept out to sea. A few hours later, another one followed suit.

The lone survivor said that he and the other man stayed with the boat until morning. That's when the third man to lose his life decided to swim for help toward a light he said he saw in the distance. He was not seen again.

I could understand the idea of being delusional, seeing a light, and thinking I could swim toward it in my desperation. But I couldn't understand how or why, one by one, the other two men could possibly take off their life jackets and allow themselves to drift out into waves to face certain death.

But now I understand. Like me wasting away in Red Hook, they were being relentlessly tortured. And in their despair they experienced true hopelessness. All their hope was gone, and now I can see it.

> *A man devoid of hope and conscious of being so has ceased to belong to the future.*
> —Albert Camus

Warning! Warning! If you have a weak stomach you may want to skip over the following until I give you the *all clear.*

Living in the shooting galleries on Columbia Avenue in Red Hook, Susan and I appeared to be in the last stages of our existence. And for those who are not street smart, when I talk about "shooting galleries" I'm not speaking of shooting ducks at the state fair or carnival with a BB gun.

A shooting gallery is where addicts gather, usually in the projects—an apartment belonging to someone who, in exchange for money and drugs, allows you to come in and shoot your drugs intravenously.

The shooting galleries had all the services an addict needed, including sex (prostitutes) and filthy spikes (syringes).The hookers there helped the drug addicts shoot up if the addicts' hands were too shaky to hit a vein. But of course, the addicts had to share their dope with the hookers for such *concierge* services.

The veins in my arms and those of Susan were calloused and collapsed from the abuse of constant injections, and were always struggling to get a hit. So like many others there in Red Hook, we resorted to shooting into veins in our necks and other parts of the body in order to administer the heroin.

We stayed there in the shooting galleries most of the time. In fact, we only left to pick up more drugs. That became the extent of our existence.

It was truly meaningless.

We slept on the floor, always with one eye open. If you closed both eyes, or blacked out, the others would raid your pockets for any money or drugs.

Not all closed eye is sleeping, nor open eye is seeing.
—Chinese proverb

I remember *Samurai*. They called him that for a reason. He was a coke freak who would stand motionless with paranoia for hours at a time in the middle of the room, staring straight ahead frozen while holding a 36 inch long samurai sword in the attack position.

We would navigate very delicately around him when moving about the room. He never flinched, never budged, never blinked. Our greatest concern was that he would thaw out without warning and go into action.

Paranoid? Probably. But just because you're paranoid doesn't mean there isn't an invisible demon about to eat your face.
—Jim Butcher

Prostitutes and other women were walking about the shooting gallery revealing themselves in sheer clothing in hopes of luring a customer into their web for drug money. However, sex, for the most part, was pointless to the addicts. All their senses were dulled. Their natural endorphins were destroyed and being impersonated by the opiates.

Females frequently came up to me if I was holding drugs and began to disrobe only to hear me shout, "Put your clothes back on!" Our drugs ruled our senses.

Pleasure for the hardcore addicts—and I use the term, pleasure, loosely—could only be produced or stimulated through heroin or cocaine, or the popular combination of the two (speedballs).

Hookers always were lurking over you in attempts to get some of your "blood" from a shot of dope, in no less a way a vampire lusts after your blood. So when you needed them to "shoot you up", they would cook up the heroin in a spoon or bottle cap, draw up the heroin into your spike (syringe), (but not all of it), and shoot it into your veins for you.

Then as the addict began to nod out from the high, she would squeeze what she had "hidden" in the spike for herself into her own spoon and shoot up her portion into her own veins, the other addict's blood and all.

Aids was beginning to rear its ugly head in the 1980s, especially in the drug culture, but no one at that time really knew what it was or where it came from.

So consequently, there was very little fear of it among the addicts, and little or no attention was given to it. Now you see a big reason why Aids and Hepatitis C became epidemic.

Vinnie, my street partner, shared needles with me on a daily basis. He actually wasted away and died of Aids. But thankfully I never contracted the disease. I chalk that up to yet another miracle that I experienced back then.

It was impossible for me not to have contracted the disease.

AIDS is such a scary thing, and it's also the kind of thing that you think won't happen to you. It can happen to you, and it's deadly serious. —Ice T

TATO BIEN; TATO BIEN; TATO BIEN. ALL CLEAR

It wasn't long after we moved into Red Hook when Susan began prostituting her body again. She did the deed on the streets of

Brooklyn under the elevated BQE near the mouth of the Brooklyn Battery Tunnel at 3rd Avenue.

That is a very popular spot where many commuters exiting the tunnel pass (and stop) on their way home to their happy little, unsuspecting wives. They are lured to stop there by the hookers; then after they get what they need there, they continue on to bring their wives flowers, candy . . . and Aids.

Susan and I walked two miles from the shooting galleries in Red Hook in the 90-degree city heat of the summer to that location every day for Susan to turn tricks. Waves of heat rose off the blacktop like a mirage as we perched ourselves on a rail waiting there for her customers.

From time to time she would jump off the rail and do her strut to attract the weak-minded motorists. That is what we did all hours of the day and night to survive. It was the only way. Well . . . not really the only way.

> *Desperation is sometimes as powerful an inspirer as genius.*
> —Benjamin Disraeli

When I was desperate for a fix, there was nothing I wouldn't do—nothing. I would bite off your finger to get to your gold. So I also joined with the "stick up boys" and committed armed robbery at Brooklyn gas stations, right in the middle of busy intersections.

We drove up in a car and asked the attendants to fill up the tank, which they did. Then as the tank was filling we got out and appeared to ready ourselves to pay for the gas.

But as the attendants removed the gas nozzle from the car, secured it away, and reached into their pockets to remove the fat wad of bills most station attendants kept in their pockets in those days to make change, we forcefully shoved a handgun up under their chins or into their temples.

We surrounded them, and while they were frozen from fright and unable to talk, we grabbed the roll of bills from them and sped off after warning them not to call the police, or we would pay them another visit.

They usually never called the police for fear of reprisal.

Crazy, right?

No. Desperate!

If we didn't get busted (and we didn't), we had enough drug money for a couple days. That is just one of the many ways we addicts supplied our daily habits. Even today, nearly three quarters of all violent crimes are drug related.

I took my share of the money, and soon I was shooting up speedballs all night long, alone, out of control, and picking *coke bugs* out of my arms and my face until morning. I was covered with sores.

Coke bugs you might ask? I thought you would.

Well, Wikipedia puts it this way:

Stimulant drug abuse (particularly amphetamine and cocaine) can lead to delusional parasitosis (aka Ekbom's Syndrome: a mistaken belief they are infested with parasites). For example, excessive cocaine use can lead to formication [with an "M" not an "N"], nicknamed "cocaine bugs" or "coke bugs," where the affected people believe they have, or feel, parasites crawling under their skin. . . . People experiencing these hallucinations might scratch themselves to the extent of serious skin damage and bleeding, especially when they are delirious.

I could see Coke bugs burrowing into my skin. Panicking, I dug aggressively into my skin with my fingernails all night as I tried to get rid of them before they entered my body.

The coke bugs were out in force, doing military maneuvers, all jazzed up on their Bolivian marching powder.

—Mark D. Diehl

Of course there were no bugs, but an addict's hallucinating mind makes a scary reality of it. My face, arms, and thighs looked like a roadmap to hell—like I was either attacked by a swarm of South American killer bees or ran through a cheese grater.

Then with ever-increasing desperation and hopelessness, I reached another low point by submitting myself to dope dealers as a human guinea pig to test the quality of their heroin. By that time it was one of the few ways left for me to get the constant fixes I needed.

It was like playing Russian Roulette. But remember, it really didn't matter to me if I OD'd and died. I knew the risk I was taking. We were already dead men walking, so what did it matter?

They would shoot me up and watch my reaction. If they saw my eyes go up into my head, that meant the heroin was high quality stuff. Then they would purchase large quantities of it, and give me my share for the day. Insane? No doubt. It's amazing what a human being will do to survive even when he doesn't care to live. It is nothing but the instinct of survival.

> *Sometimes even to live is an act of courage.* — *Seneca*

One day after returning from the streets, as we entered the shooting gallery on Columbia Avenue we saw that the solid metal front door to the apartment was riddled with bullet holes. It turned out that the bullet holes were put there by a police Swat Team who burst through the door looking for one of our *friends*.

I thought it was a drug bust, and we were all going to be rounded up and locked up. However, they were not looking for small fish like us. They were looking for Gumby. Yes, *Gumby*. Let me explain.

While we were gone, one of our group had flipped out on cocaine. He was completely paranoid and went to Long Island to kidnap the wife of a rich businessman. Which he did!

The Swat Team grilled all of us, but we didn't know where he was. (Of course we wouldn't have told them even if we did.) They roughed us up a bit in their search, and then left without making any arrests. They ignored the heroin and drug paraphernalia in the apartment and walked quickly out the door.

Kidnapping is a federal offense. They wanted the kidnapper, not a bunch of small-time drug addicts. If New York City jailed every small-time criminal in town, they would have to build twelve more prisons.

Well, after several days, guess who was on the front page of the New York City Daily News? That's right! Our boy "Gumby"— picked up and arrested by New York's finest, and wearing his infamous "Gumby" T-shirt. Hence, we nicknamed him Gumby. Well, Gumby didn't look very happy. He was facing big time in prison, and we never saw Gumby again.

Gumby was a gentle and passive twenty-five-year-old. But like so many, his addiction brought him to that day of insanity. Addiction will compel an individual to act against his conscience. And the longer he ignores his conscience the more seared it becomes. It loses all sensitivity to life. And he eventually becomes another *Dead Man Walking*.

Disease, danger, even death—nothing concerned us.

We'd stared into the face of Death, and Death blinked first. You'd think that would make us feel brave and invincible. It didn't. —Rick Yancey, The 5th Wave

One night, my street buddy, Larry L., and I (we watched each other's back) were on our way in a car to cop some dope with Jose, a friend of ours in the back seat. Again, I use the term "friend" very loosely. Jose was the man with the money. He still worked a job and had just been paid, so we didn't let him out of our sight.

As we drove down the street we realized it was really quiet in the back seat. We turned around and saw that Jose was blue—and I mean BLUE. He had overdosed in the back seat while Larry and I were talking.

You might assume in a situation like that we would make an emergency stop and call 911, but ... are you crazy? We were on another mission. And being "on a mission" seemed to give an addict a sense of purpose. Purpose! What a joke.

Code Blue! We were not concerned with Jose's life; we were interested in his money. But we were concerned about what kind of trouble having a dead man in the back seat of our car might bring to us. That's pretty-much how seared a conscience can become.

While I continued driving, Larry turned to face the back seat, got up on his knees, and started smacking Jose's face back and forth like Mohammad Ali hitting Joe Frazier in the *Thrilla in Manila*. After two or three minutes of that Jose started breathing again. His face was pretty swollen, but he came out of it like nothing happened.

We continued down the street and copped our dope with the blue man's money. Experiences like that just marked another day in the life on an addict.

There is a thin line on the streets between life and death.

Considering how dangerous everything is, nothing is really very frightening. —Gertrude Stein

You always have to watch your back on the streets. I often walked through the streets of Brooklyn at three and four in the morning going into drug houses. I could have had my throat slit many times. To protect myself in that environment I always carried an extended kitchen blade up my right sleeve. To stay prepared I practiced by quickly throwing my arm forward and catching the blade in my hand.

Our lives were constantly in danger on the streets in Red Hook. A person could be safer on the front lines of a war zone in Iraq than in those streets in the early morning hours.

Danger can only be overcome by more danger —Greek proverb

On one hot, humid day with temperatures in the upper nineties, Susan and I left the projects on our daily survival "mission trip." We never knew where we would wind up. All we knew was we would do whatever was necessary to get our fix throughout that day and night. Thin and suffering from malnutrition, our minds were so severely affected that the struggle of daily survival was becoming more than we could bear.

We came to an abandoned building where some addicts were living. We were both dehydrated, so we went into the building to get out of the searing sun. Once in the building we found a couple who was willing to turn us on to some of their cocaine.

We cooked up the cocaine and "banged" it (which means we injected it all with one quick thrust), and my heart suddenly began to race out of control. Cocaine is a powerful stimulant and it will always increase a person's heart rate. We were familiar with that effect and looked forward to the energy it brought to us. But that time it was different. I couldn't breathe, and I knew I was going into respiratory arrest.

I immediately ran outside to get air and prayed a panic prayer to God. You know, it was one of those when you lie and tell God that if He keeps you from dying you will never use drugs again (which seems kind of strange when you think about it, since I didn't think I cared if I lived or died).

I was bent over on the sidewalk, saying loudly, "Please don't let me die here in the street. Please, God. Not here in the street".

Then someone from inside ran out with some pills and told me to take them quickly and chew them up. I didn't have any idea what they were. But I didn't care at the time, so I took them. Slowly I began to be able to breathe, and before long I was once again breathing calmly.

You might think that after that near fatal overdose I would go back to the projects. But the addiction to cocaine is so powerful that, within just minutes of that near fatal episode, I went back into the building to do more cocaine.

Like heroin, cocaine has a powerful will of its own. It too will deplete your will. It will control your mind and everything you do. I could not stop consuming it.

Yet I survived to live another day. And why? So I could go on another mission.

Why? I was a dead man walking.

In the final phase of cocaine intoxication, when suicide is likely, the victim cannot save himself by an effort of will. He has lost the power. —Carroll O'Connor

CHAPTER 14

I ONLY SPIT IN BROOKLYN

Have you ever seen a dead possum in the road that has been run over by a car? In New York we call them "flat rats."

Well, that's what we looked like and that is the way we felt, like a flat rat.

We were filthy and hungry as Susan and I walked down 4th Avenue in Brooklyn after copping some dope for our morning fix. And we were soaking wet from being caught in a thunderstorm. As usual, we were both sick and in deep withdrawal. Emaciated and barely able to walk, we knew we couldn't make it back to the shooting gallery.

We had to have our fix! We were in a state of panic as we looked for any place at all where we could shoot our heroin. It couldn't wait; we were severely nauseated and ready to collapse.

Fourth Avenue in Brooklyn is a wide street with a divider between the uptown and downtown lanes of traffic. And the center divider is landscaped with a variety of bushes and small trees in some of the wider sections of the street. It was still raining as we walked between the lanes of traffic, when we spotted two large bushes next to each other in the center divider.

We usually looked for a local bathroom to slip into and shoot up (a favorite place of drug addicts), but that wasn't an option. In New York City they are few and far between, and the business owners are street wise to the local addicts. So we climbed in between the two bushes, and with traffic racing to and fro on both sides of us, we shot our dope.

Welcome to the life of a heroin addict.

Soaking wet, filthy, and weak, we began walking down 4th Avenue again. Then suddenly Susan walked over to the curb and spit into the gutter.

I became furious.

Even as depraved a life I was living—even with Susan selling her body to get our drugs—believe it or not, I have always been disgusted by a female who would spit—especially spitting in public. The spitting infuriated me, not the prostitution. Can you imagine that? Strange value system.

It's okay for you to sell your body, but don't spit!

I guess it must have been the last fiber of dignity that I was holding on to. I always believed a woman should act with dignity.

I was out of control. I snapped. I grabbed Susan violently by the arm, shook her, and began screaming at the top of my lungs right there in the middle of 4th Avenue.

"Don't you ever let me see you spit in public in front of me again!"

She began crying, weeping violently out of control. Then she said something to me that I will never forget.

She said, "I only spit in Brooklyn."

It had nothing to do with Brooklyn. It had everything to do with the world we had created for ourselves. And this dark painful cold isolated world we created happened to be located in Brooklyn. A world where no one could see us because no one cared enough to see us.

Brooklyn became The Underworld.

She said, I only spit in Brooklyn, because Susan felt she had lost her identity as a human being—her self worth as a woman—in Brooklyn. So it didn't matter if she sold her body, it didn't matter if she shot dope in the public bushes, it didn't matter if she *spit* in the gutter, it didn't matter if she died—no one would know. No one cared.

She only spit in Brooklyn.

> *To the last, I grapple with thee; from Hell's heart, I stab at thee;*
> *for hate's sake, I spit my last breath at thee.*
>
> —Herman Melville

Susan and I both had lost all sense of decency and self-esteem. We survived like mere animals. After running the Five Bouroughs of New York City in self-destruct mode, it was Brooklyn where we were ready to die without hope.

For me, I felt like I was with Custer at his *Last Stand*. Only Susan and I were not bravely ending our lives fighting against our enemy. We were just broken-down shells of what we once were, and neither of us felt like fighting anymore.

It could have been anywhere, but Brooklyn is where we hit rock bottom. End of the line. We looked and felt like those flat rats.

Life without meaning, life without purpose, and life with no future—it isn't life at all. There was no way out of the pit we had been digging for ourselves. It was too deep. We were trapped with no way of escape.

It was hopeless. There was no possibility of finding a solution.

The whole thing is quite hopeless, so it's no good worrying about tomorrow. It probably won't come.   — *J.R.R. Tolkien*

CHAPTER 15

CAGED

Still alive, but just barely, and in desperation, I reached out to one of my former bookmaking customers for some money he owed me. I did it for Susan. I could not watch her suffer.

With my mind clouded but my manipulating genius still at peak efficiency, I threatened to expose him to the mob for cheating on his bets if he didn't pay me what he owed me. (It was yet another of my Academy Award performances.) The man was a person of position and reputation, and he quickly made arrangements for a money transfer directly to Susan.

> *A wise man knows everything; a shrewd one, everybody.*
> —Unknown Author

I then contacted my son to come back and take Susan to Jersey for the pick-up. The police were on high alert for me in New Jersey, so I would not enter the state.

(I am still not certain to this day how the following all transpired, but here it is:)

While in Jersey with my son, Susan went to my sister's house where our daughter was. Susan demanded to see Tiffani, but my sister had received temporary custody and hesitated to let her touch Tiffani out of caution. But Susan was as cunning as I was, and after deceiving my sister with a kiss, she swept Tiffani up and bolted for the car.

As withdrawal began to set in on her, she took the wheel of the car from my son, and raced wildly to make the meeting for the money transfer. Getting weaker and sick, she began to nod off at the wheel and slammed broadside into a city bus, injuring both herself and my daughter and my son.

That was not in New York, so the Jersey police were immediately investigating the accident. And word of the accident got back to me (don't ask me how) while I was still in a shooting gallery in Red Hook.

When I heard that my little baby girl, three and a half years old at the time, had been in a serious accident, I lost what little mind I had left. My will to live briefly returned when I heard that my little girl was in trouble, and I immediately started running down to the street on impulse. I ran onto Columbia Avenue and waved down a private cab. (There were no Yellow Cabs in that risky neighborhood.)

The driver was a woman, and I explained to her what happened and that I must to go to Jersey, and now!

A crazy person can be very persuasive.

The driver asked for payment. I had no money, so I conned her (or frightened her to death, perhaps) into believing that I would pick up the money at our destination. I promised to pay her there.

Rigggght!

Here's rule number one in Drug Education: "Never believe a drug addict."

So she raced down to Jersey with a madman lurking over her shoulder in her backseat. Believe me, I looked like I had just escaped from the Rikers Island psych ward after a shock treatment.

> *Voluntarily inflicted a certain level of insanity on myself.*
> —Jonathan Franzen

I hadn't been in Jersey for years, and my mind was so disoriented that I couldn't remember where the "hospital on the Garden State Parkway" was. (That is the information I was given; I wasn't told the name of the hospital. It's Bayshore Community.) I could only remember that it was right off the Garden State Parkway.

So at about five o'clock in the morning, there I was in Jersey, out of control, looking for a hospital in a New York private taxi.

"Stop!" I shouted. "There it is. I see it! It's over there."

There was one problem, though. We were in a south-bound lane, and the hospital was on Parkway North, with the north and south lanes separated by a large grassy median at least twenty-five to thirty yards wide containing trees and bushes.

"Stop!" commanded the madman in the back seat. And she stopped out of shear fear.

I then bolted out of the taxi as she screamed, "Where's my money?!"

I ran faster and never looked back.

I ran straight across the parkway's southbound lanes like a gazelle running from a hungry lion (at least I thought I was running straight). I ran across the grassy knoll, across the northbound lanes, and right to the rear of the hospital.

Anyone who saw me must have thought it was the ever-elusive Jersey Devil.

Well, at least I thought I was at the hospital. In my panic and confusion I ran at a 45 degree angle straight into a neighboring professional building. And guess what I found there? It was a young man unchaining his bicycle (poor soul), getting ready to go on his newspaper delivery route.

(I have a feeling you're already getting ahead of me.) Must I say more?

Many people did not get their newspapers that day.

I asked him where the hospital was, and he answered with a question, "Bayshore?"

I said, "Is that the name of the Hospital?"

"Yes," he answered. "Bayshore Community Hospital is just the next building about a quarter mile north of here."

I then told him I needed his bicycle, and that it wasn't optional.

No one in his right mind should argue with a man at five-something in the morning, who just ran across the Garden State Parkway looking like he had just been transformed into wolf man by the moon.

The young man was scared straight. He didn't resist. And he was a smart boy.

So off I went up Parkway North on his bicycle until I came to Bayshore Hospital, which has a parkway access road. I threw the bicycle down and raced into the main entrance. At about 5:30 a.m., with the sun just coming up, I burst into the lobby, marched up to the desk, and demanded, "I want to see my daughter!"

Now you must get the full picture, here.

First, it was not exactly visiting hours. And in walks this crazed, filthy, smelly lunatic demanding to see his daughter. Oh, by the way, did I forget to mention there with syringes sticking up out of my top shirt pocket like fountain pens. (That's the way we walked around in the streets of Red Hook.)

Oh, and did I also forget to tell you in my pocket were several bags (small glassine bags) of heroin?

Getting the picture. My mind was still in the projects.

> *Insanity—it's difficult to comprehend how insane some people can be. Especially when you're insane.*
>
> —Larry Kersten

So there I was, looking like I just escaped from a maximum security prison, demanding to see my daughter. The desk receptionist was probably scared to death. But she was nice to me, too nice (if you know what I mean) and said, "Please wait, and we will make arrangements for you to see her."

So I waited, and I waited. And I waited, and I waited. Then I waited some more. After some time passed I was getting my Italian "rabbia" up, and I was expressing my displeasure with some choice Italian slang that definitely would have offended them if they had understood Italian.

Then it finally hit me, "You can't act like that in Jersey at 5:30 in the morning!"

They were stalling me. (And I thought I was so street wise . . . Stunad!) And just as I realized that, I turned around to start running . . . but too late.

The hospital doors blasted open, and the Holmdel, New Jersey police burst in, grabbed me, restrained me, ripped the syringes and heroin out of my pockets, threw me to the floor, and cuffed my hands behind my back.

(While on the ground I managed to grab one bag of heroin and tightly closed my fist on it.)

They then picked me up, threw me into the back seat of a patrol car, and went back into the lobby to question the attendants.

There I was again—back in familiar wrist-jewelry.

I was panicking. I knew I would never get out of jail if they locked me up in Jersey. I had years' worth of warrants out on me in New Jersey. I struggled and wrestled in the back seat of the patrol car to get my cuffed hands through my legs and in front of me.

From my warped perception, I was fighting for my life, so anything goes. I thought if I could get my hands in front of me, I could kick out the safety divider that separated the front of the police car from the back, jump over the seat, and race off in the car.

I had to get out of Jersey and back to New York. Once there, no one would ever find me. That was my mentality.

But that wasn't meant to be. I struggled, but I couldn't get my arms through. I was exhausted. But I still held onto the bag of dope in my hand. I knew I would need it soon.

Soon the police came out of the hospital and took me to the local station's holding pen. I knew I had to make bail fast. And I knew it had to be a quick bail, because I had so many outstanding charges against me in the state—including charges for absconding probation years earlier.

I was a cooked goose if I didn't get bail before they transferred me to Monmouth County Jail in Freehold. Once in Freehold they would identify me as a crime figure and make bail impossible.

Remember, years earlier I was a key figure in the NY/NJ gambling probes. I had been questioned by a grand jury, and they would enjoy having me back in the palms of their hands.

So what did I do? I called my former bosses and pleaded with them to bail me out QUICKLY!

The top man, whom I will not identify even though he is now deceased, wanted nothing to do with me. I was dangerous in their eyes, and I could implicate them in a drug scandal. But one of the under bosses who was close to me before said he would come with bail. But he couldn't come until the next morning.

I pleaded with him, "That will be too late! By then I'll be transferred to MCCI, and things will get much more complicated. I have to make bail here at the local police station. And I have to make it now!"

I called the top man again. He was furious with me. I begged. But again they said they would send a bail bondsman down in the morning. They didn't want to appear and show any association with me.

I felt like a caged animal, and morning came too late. Before the bail bondsman arrived I was transferred to Monmouth County Correctional Institution, and the process I feared began. Former and present charges began to pile. After nine different charges were filed against me my bail went from a simple $250 in the Holmdel police station to close to $200,000 at MCCI.

Now I became poison to the bookmakers. There is no honor among thieves. They were afraid that I would talk if they didn't bail me out; but then on the other hand, if they did bail me out, they publicly associated themselves with me and my association with drugs.

So there I sat—in the "welcome home" cage of MCCI. (I was well known there.) But at that moment, being in jail was the least of my troubles. Real trouble was about to begin. My withdrawal symptoms were beginning to set in.

I was placed in F wing with my fellow "animals"—I mean inmates. They were at first cautious to come near me. They thought I might have Aids. And of course I had to have smelled like a female buffalo in heat.

They laid me in a bunk, and I lay there unconscious for two days. I was twisting, turning, and crawling out of my skin for forty-eight hours. Then the other inmates sweated the dope out of me by throwing me into hot showers and keeping me there.

> *I got to grow up in a situation where drugs were demonic. To watch your dad go through heroin withdrawal is something that would keep you from doing any of that yourself.*
> —Shia LaBeouf

When you were in jail in the 80's with no detox medication offered to you, you have no choice but to suffer through the withdrawals.

Again, my fellow animals (there I go again) I mean inmates, would force me (I had no choice) back into the shower and make me eat some chocolate to get my strength back little by little.

I could not eat for days, but slowly I forced myself to walk to the mess hall in an attempt to get needed nourishment. I sat alone most of the time. Many still were convinced I carried disease, and in those days everyone had become fearful of Aids.

I began to regain some strength after several weeks, and I also started to regain my ability for shrewdness. My experienced, scheming mind once again began to kick into high gear. I wanted out. I wanted to get out of Jersey and get back to New York. But how could I get $200,000 cash bail?

Hmmmmm . . . let me think . . .

CHAPTER 16

THE TWILIGHT ZONE

"My uncle! My naïve Uncle B." The thought suddenly burst upon me.

"Yeah! My uncle is closest kin to my mother, and he owns a house. I'm sure he has more than $200,000 worth of equity in his house. It might even be paid off. There's my bail money!"

I planned to go to work on his emotions. With a good con and some expertly flavored manipulative words, I was sure I could win him over. After all, he wouldn't lose his house if he put it up as collateral for my bail . . . or would he?

> *The basic tool for the manipulation of reality is the manipulation of words. If you can control the meaning of words, you can control the people who must use the words.* —Philip K. Dick

I had two problems though. I didn't know my uncle's phone number. And it's nearly impossible to make telephone calls from MCCI in the 1980's.

Unlike today, when the phones are inside prison wings and can pretty-much be used liberally, in 1987 the phones were outside of the wing and out of reach by the prisoners. Inmates had to put their names on a phone "wish" list and wait in line to be called one by one by the typically unfriendly guard who came, at his convenience, to work the phones.

The phones were only available for short periods of time during the day and evening. And if there was an inmate in line who was bigger and stronger than you, the phone list had little meaning.

After days of waiting, I finally made it to the phone. I stood there with a clouded mind, struggling to recall my uncle's number, but it was to no avail. So I decided to call my sister and hope she would give it to me.

Oops . . . stop! I nearly forgot. I had robbed her house twice. It wasn't a good idea to call her at this time.

Finally, I decided to call my cousin Rena. She lived in Manhattan in a classy Upper East Side neighborhood. And believe me, she was also classy. It's a good thing she was my cousin, or I would have hit on her long ago. (I did think about it, though.)

La famiglia even rented her apartment location for major gambling operations at one time (one of the places where I operated a bookmaking office). And even though I robbed her house, too, (remember the rule, never trust a heroin addict) she would forgive me, I hoped.

If you know a heroin addict, never let him into your house—not for a moment. He is a magician. He can make anything disappear right before your eyes. And if you sleep with your mouth open, you may be missing your dentures in the morning if any gold was used in their construction.

When a thief kisses you, count your teeth.—Yiddish Proverb

So I dialed up my cousin Rena.

"The line's busy!" I said in my frustration. "After waiting days to get to the phone . . . the line's busy. @#%*#@*&%$!"

I could only use the phone for five minutes. I was getting frustrated.

I called again, and . . . "Busy again! #@&^*%$#@%!"

My five minutes were up, and I was returned to my jail wing by the guard.

"Okay, don't get frustrated. Settle down. There is always tomorrow," I tried to reason with myself.

Now there was another dynamic at play in addition to all the other reasons why I needed to get out of jail as soon as possible. There was another reason I needed to make bail as soon as possible so I could once again vanish into the streets of Brooklyn.

You see, I was walking on thin ice with the New Jersey probation office. I was still officially on probation in Jersey as a result of charges brought against me years ago. I had absconded, which means I skipped town, never reported, and disappeared. But law enforcement officials are very wise and patient. They know that sooner or later a criminal will surface again, and they will have their day.

Now when an individual absconds probation, they are violated and a warrant is put out for their arrest. I knew that if I was ever arrested in New Jersey again, the probation office would be alerted and I would have a "detainer" (the word speaks for itself) placed on me.

That means ... NO BAIL. It means ... I'm cooked.

Actually, I couldn't understand why a detainer had not already been placed on me. It didn't make sense. Day after day I checked with the guards to see if one had been filed, and each day I was told there was still no detainer. Because of that, I knew I could still make bail. So I stepped up my attempts at manipulating my way out of jail.

Time was of the essence though. I knew eventually the detainer was coming. But when? If it came after I made bail I would be home free.

I made it to the phone again on the next day. "This time I'll get through to Rena and get my uncle's phone number," I thought.

"Busy . . . busy . . . busy again! What's going on? Okay, calm down; I have five minutes."

I dialed again, and still it was busy.

"Okay, okay, relax." I talked to myself. "You are a master manipulator. You'll work this out. No jail can hold you too long." (Riiiiiiight.)

The third day came. "Busy . . . busy . . . busy!"

The fourth day came, and I fought to get on the phone list. I failed.

I was really getting frustrated by the fifth day. "Busy . . . busy . . . busy, again!"

> *The torment of human frustration, whatever its immediate cause, is the knowledge that the self is in prison, its vital force and "mangled mind" leaking away in lonely, wasteful self-conflict.*
> —Elizabeth Drew

On day six I thought I would get through for certain. I dialed.

"Busy . . . busy . . . busy!"

By then I was nearly going insane. "This can't be happening. She's the only one who can give me my uncle's phone number! How can a number be busy day after day, time after time, even when I am attempting to call at different times of the day?"

> *I feel as if I were a piece in a game of chess, when my opponent says of it: That piece cannot be moved.* —Soren Kierkegaard

On day seven, after getting yet another busy signal, I quickly decided to change my plan. I decided to call my goombah, a former associate of mine from the family.

I decided to call him before my time for the phone that day ran out and ask him to contact my cousin Rena for me from the outside since my time on the phone was so limited.

So I called him, and what I discovered shook me up.

Remember, I was checking every day with the guards to see if a detainer had been filed on me yet by the probation department. If they filed a detainer I was looking at possibly fifteen years in jail. I was becoming more and more anxious, but every day the detainer wasn't filed was another day I could use trying to make bail.

I couldn't understand why it wasn't filed on me immediately after I entered incarceration. It didn't make sense, but although I still couldn't understand it, I continued to take advantage of every day by frantically attempting to contact my uncle. I knew it was just a matter of time before the detainer would be filed if I didn't make bail. I had to escape from Jersey!

So my goombah answered the phone right away, and I asked him to call my cousin for me.

He immediately said, "You stunod, that's not her number! You've been calling the wrong number."

I was speechless, stunned. I was calling the wrong number for a week. But what got to me even more is that I could not comprehend a working number being constantly busy. It was a working number, yet it was continuously busy day after day after day, throughout the day, at different times of the day. That was more than a little strange.

A very interesting time line had begun.

If the people had just answered the phone they could have told me I had the wrong number, and I wouldn't have wasted all that valuable time. I knew there was no time to lose.

My time with the telephone for that day ran out, but I had the right telephone number. So on day eight I called my cousin Rena, finally made contact with her, and asked her to forgive me. She was cool even though I had robbed her house blind, and she gave me my uncle's telephone number.

Things were finally looking better for me. Next I would call my uncle; he would bail me out by putting his house up as security; and then I would race back to Brooklyn, melt into the environment, and never be seen again.

That was my ingenious plan.

Only two things are infinite, the universe and human stupidity, and I'm not sure about the former. —Albert Einstein

The next day came. It was day nine.

"Hello, Uncle B? This is Ronn. Yes, I know. It's been a long time. I need to tell you I'm really sorry about this, but I got myself into a difficult situation. I was gambling, and the police arrested me."

I love him, but he was an easy mark.

"Please Uncle B, don't let me stay in here with all these criminals." I was doing my best to produce another award winning Hollywood performance as I continued. "And you know that my mother, if she were alive, would be devastated and never allow me to remain in this terrible place (sob, sob)."

My mother had recently passed away and he was very close to her. "Do it for her, Uncle. Do it for her."

I even managed a few tears. And my performance was so good that I even imagined hearing an audience giving me a standing ovation as I went on playing my role.

My uncle hesitated at first . . . and hesitated. Then he asked, "How much is the bail?"

I responded, "Oh, only a measly two hundred thou."

He went off like he had blown a stitch in the hernia operation he just had.

"Calm down Uncle, calm down. It's very simple. This can be done with no cash. Simply place your home as security. And after the court matter is settled you are freed from the contract of bail, and all security paperwork is returned to you."

"Please Uncle, think of my mother."Sob, sob.

I had him then. He agreed to guarantee my bail and told me he would come down to the county courthouse in the morning.

You are a manipulator. I like to think of myself more as an outcome engineer.
                                                          —J.R. Ward

"Ahhhh, I'm free! Back to Brooklyn. Back to my dope. back to my people. Sure he'll lose his house, but he's financially secure."

His house was history. I had no conscience. To me his house was not worth fifteen years of my life. I wanted out of there and would do anything to get back to New York, fast.

The following morning came. It was day ten in the saga, and I was packed and ready to leave. I was pacing the floor of F wing like a hungry cheetah.

"Still no detainer?" I asked the guard.

"Yes! Still no detainer."

But also, still no uncle.

On day eleven I'm thinking, "He'll be here today."

Still no uncle. I was growing more frustrated by the minute.

On day twelve I was back on the telephone. "Uncle, what happened?"

"I was on my way," he responded, "and I was halfway there when something told me to turn around and go back home."

"Something told you? Something told you? What told you?" I was livid and panicking.

Then I entered my final performance—a masterful one even if I do say so myself.

"Uncle," I pleaded, sobbing a few more tears (that were actually easier to produce that time), "please don't leave me here in this forsaken place. Please. Remember my mother!"

That final act did it.

"Okay, I'll come. I'll come there tomorrow."

"Please don't disappoint me again," I said.

"I won't," he responded before hanging up the phone. "I'll definitely be there."

"Halleluiah! Halleluiah! I'm out," I said to myself. "And on a Friday night! I'll be in Brooklyn getting high again. Jersey will never see me again. Sorry about your house, Uncle. But you can always buy another one. Easy come, easy go."

Then, quickly, I checked with the guards about the detainer. There still was no detainer. I couldn't understand it, but I gladly received the news. That news still made it possible for me to receive my free ticket out of Jersey.

Nevertheless, I felt uneasy. Everything that was happening was so strange: the episodes with getting to the phone; calling the wrong number that was busy for over a week; my uncle turning around and going back home because "something" told him to; the probation department silent when I was within their grasp; it was all very, very strange.

Friday, day thirteen, arrived, and I was ready and listening to hear the guard call my name followed by "ETG" (Everything To Go). My uncle was coming after work, and I expected him to arrive at about 5:00 p.m.. I estimated I would make it back to Brooklyn just in time to . . . parr-tayy!

Six o'clock in the evening rolled around, and I thought excitedly, "Okay, they must be filling out all the paperwork downstairs."

At 7:00 p.m.: No uncle

At 7:30 p.m. there was still no uncle. And I was beginning to worry.

I was nervously sitting there with my little sack packed with all my life's belongings and listening for my number to be called, and then it happened.

"Here comes the guard. I'm free! I'm free!".

I was waiting to hear him say that coveted acronym "ETG," but the guard came up to me and whispered, "There's some confusion. There is a delay. We have a bit of confusion downstairs."

"Confusion?" I responded

"At the same time your uncle arrived and began completing bail papers for your release," he whispered to me, "an officer from the probation department also arrived. He arrived at the very same moment as your uncle."

"Noooooooo!"

It turned out that his senior probation officer sent him to the jail after-hours, on a Friday night, right before the weekend, after returning from vacation and spotting my name as an arrest.

"Your uncle had just completed filling out your bail papers," said the guard. "He stopped your uncle in his tracks and placed a detainer on you."

I was stunned motionless.

Then I lost it and started shouting. "This is crazy! This is crazy!" I shouted at the top of my lungs.

They were about to lock me up in solitary, but the guard intervened. However, I continued to shout. "What's going on? What's happening?!

"What the %$$@*&$ is going on?!"

The time line of all those events was too perfect to be a natural event. I knew it couldn't have just all been a string of coincidences. From day one something strange was developing.

Trouble getting to the phones; trouble recalling my cousin's number after working out of her home for years; calling a wrong number numerous times that was constantly busy; my uncle canceling the first time he was supposed to get me out because "something" told him to turn around . . .

The senior probation officer being on vacation and getting back the same day I was to be released; his decision to send one of his officers to the jail after normal hours; the probation officer's after-hours arrival at the exact moment my uncle finally came to my rescue . . .

It all just blew my mind!

"Could all this be a coincidence?" I thought. "No; the timing of the sequence of events was too perfect. Was it designed? Did someone actually write a script, and I've really just been acting it out? Am I crazy? No!"

It was like I was acting in an episode of *The Twilight Zone*. But all those stories were just made up. They were fabricated out of the mind of their writer, Rod Serling. But what I was then experiencing was real life, right?

"Aha, I must be dreaming. I must be caught up in a nightmare! This must be a nightmare, a bad dream. Surely I'll wake up, and it will be over."

My mind couldn't comprehend how that nightmare situation could be anything but an unnatural event. If it were real, it had to be orchestrated, right? Yes, it had to be. But by whom? Or by what?

Then I heard it. I heard two words.

"It's Me."

I was petrified. I froze in fear. And then I heard it again.

"It's Me."

That wasn't natural. I was completely straight. I wasn't high. My mind wasn't in the cloud of drugs.

"This is crazy," I thought. "I must be going crazy. I'm hearing voices, but not with my ears. I hear it, but not with my ears. Is that possible?"

"It's Me. Me who? Who is *me?*"

"That's it. That's it. Okay . . . okay. Finally, it's happened. I've lost my mind entirely. I've cracked. I'm looney. That's it; I'm a loony!"

My head was pounding.

I wanted to run, but where? Something inside of me kept lifting my head up.

I knew that I knew, that I knew that what happened was no coincidence. But I was afraid to look up. I was frightened to death to look up.

"Who is this, *me?* God?".

"I don't know God. I never knew God. I'm not looking for any God."

"None of this makes any sense. I'm a loony!"

"No!" There was no other explanation.

I went over it again and again in my mind. I went over it all a hundred times in my mind. And every time I did, I saw a perfect sequence of events. The time line was mind-boggling, and I couldn't escape from it.

"The timing was perfect. And something turned my uncle around the first time. But what?"

"It was a plan. It was a plan to keep me in jail. But whose plan? God's?"

God? Give me a break. Something or *someone* was keeping me from being released until the detainer could be placed to remove any possibility of my release. I just didn't know what that *something* or who that *someone* was.

I found out later that the senior probation officer, who had been away on vacation for twelve days, finally returned and he decided to stop in his office to simply check his computer before leaving for the weekend. That's when he "just happened" to spot my *infamous* name.

He had been chasing me for years.

He entertained the thought of waiting until Monday before serving the detainer, but "something inside him" (here we go again) told him to send an officer after normal working hours (which was highly unusual—especially on a Friday evening) to serve the detainer on his way home.

There were exactly twelve days of delays and "coincidences" before I was able to finally get my uncle to arrive at the jail. And if that wasn't enough, both my uncle and the probation officer filing the detainer arrived at the jail at the same time on the thirteenth day!

If—if only my uncle had come the first time.

If only I could have recalled a telephone number that I had called thousands of times. (Now get this: it was not only my cousin's number but also one of the bookmaking numbers I operated from. How in the world could I have forgotten it?)

If only the wrong number I was calling hadn't been busy for seven straight days. If only the people with that phone number had picked up and answered.

If only my uncle had arrived just one day earlier.

If only my uncle hadn't been caught up in traffic he could have arrived one HOUR earlier.

IF . . . IF . . . IF.

However, *IF* there had been a change in any of those events, and *IF* my bail were to have been posted a day, an hour, or just a moment sooner, I would have bolted from that jail and quickly disappeared back into the drug culture of Red Hook.

And IF—If I had, it would no doubt have been for the last time.

A change in any of those events would have changed the critical time line of events that brought me to where I am today. A change to that time line, and I wouldn't be writing this book. My life would be entirely different today; and, in fact, it probably would have ended in death.

I finally decided that the God who people talked about must have had something to do with what I had gone through during that arrest and jail time.

This One who identified Himself as "It's Me". I'll never forget what I heard.

"It's Me".

I was clearly convinced that what I had been through wasn't a natural event. It couldn't be. But I couldn't help but ask:

"But why? Why me?"

"Of the seven billion people on the planet, this God is "talkin' to me?"

"Riggggght."

I was never a church-goer. I went only to weddings, and that was for the food afterwards. And occasionally, as a young teen or pre-teen, I would stop in Mt Carmel church—a local, popular Catholic church—to find out when the next CBA dance was, so I could hit on the girls.

Clearly I was never religious, and I knew nothing about God. I guess I always believed there had to be somebody up there who could control things—you know, some higher power somewhere up in the stars. But I was totally ignorant of what that someone could be like.

So why, you might ask, was I so sure those events were not a coincidence? How could I be so certain this God I heard about was involved in all of it? I didn't know how I knew, then. And I still don't. I can't explain it. I just knew.

And suddenly, in an instant, a strange calm came over me. The crazed man was quieted. I no longer cared about hearing the guard say, "ETG"—or about being released. I was still confused and frightened. In fact, I was petrified because I felt like something supernatural had just intervened in my life. But even while feeling fear, I still felt a calmness that I couldn't explain.

I also had another strange sense come over me. I knew something in me had changed, and I felt as if I was being "observed" by more than just the guards.

> *Man with all his shrewdness is as stupid about understanding by himself the mysteries of God, as an ass is incapable of understanding musical harmony.*   —John Calvin

There in the county prison was a man heavily addicted to every drug known on the planet, who had the morals of a hyena and the heart of a shark, and he was cowering in his jail cell, deathly afraid to look up.

No, I didn't snap. No, I wasn't going stir-crazy and hallucinating. And no, I wasn't tripping from drug flashbacks. Something happened to me, and it was real. Something of spiritual origin was beginning to stir in me. There was no other explanation.

Yes, something happened to me that was real. And it was frightening.

I could have kissed it off as another of the many coincidences and said "everything happens to me"—and then continue in my manipulating ways through the jail system like I had done so many times before.

Remember, in 1979 I had no problem being incarcerated, and had plenty of drugs brought in to me. So what happened to me? What was different this time? What did I hear? Who did I hear? What did I experience?

Whatever happened, and regardless of how or why it happened, it suddenly altered my thinking.

I may not have known anything about God at the time, but I did know about what a lot of convicts call the "Jesus freaks." The Jesus freaks were always trying to convert the other convicts. And I knew about some of those jailhouse conversions that lasted until the newly converted convict heard a guard call his name and say "ETG."

But no one had tried a jail-house conversion on me.

I was confused. And I remember being concerned that God— or whoever or whatever He was—might hit me with another whammy any minute. I was too frightened to look up.

So I quietly and cautiously went about each day in jail. (which was just not like me) I spent my days staying away from everyone else, lying in my bunk, and trying to figure out what had happened—until one day when things started changing.

One day, another inmate, who was always carrying a Bible, seemed to be tailing me as I was walking outside my cell. I didn't like it. I then noticed he was following me all the time, and I was wondering why. I tried to avoid him as much as possible. But everywhere I went, he went. He even followed me to the mess hall and sat at my table.

We never said a word to each other. Wherever he sat at the table, I sat at the extreme opposite end. But I couldn't shake the guy. I started thinking he might be an undercover FBI agent, a jail informant, or a police plant trying to get information from me on organized crime.

I wouldn't talk to that dude or even look at him. And his Bible scared the hell out of me (just telling it like it was). I associated it with the God I didn't know, the one who had just hit me with a Joe Frazier-like left hook from out of nowhere—the punch that knocked me right off my return path to New York.

Yet, the guy continued tailing me.

"Is this just one of those inmates who won't get out of my face, or what?" I thought.

All God's angels come to us disguised.—James Russell Lowell

I really think that if he hadn't carried that Bible everywhere he went, I probably would have reduced him in size by 3 inches. But I was afraid of confronting him because of that Bible.

Then one day in the mess hall he passed a note to me about a Bible study in the jail.

"This joker has to be kidding," I thought. "I don't want to go near anything associated with God. Don't you know what this

God just did to me? I was on the verge of being a free man, and He took away my freedom."

But at the same time I was resisting God, I could not overcome the curiosity that was, by that time, consuming my mind to discover who this God was and why He wacked me.

In jail, Bible-toting was a sign of weakness, so I didn't want to associate myself with those people. Nevertheless, my curiosity eventually got the better of me, and after two weeks I slipped, incognito, into the back of a meeting room where one of the guy's religious classes was about to begin.

I stood up against the back wall (I was too *bad* to sit down). I stood there wearing my long, black beard and with my arms folded. I saw myself as just an observer, not a participant. And I wanted to make sure everyone knew it.

Soon, in walked a man who couldn't have been more than five feet six inches tall, and who didn't look like any priest I was expecting from a Catholic church. As a matter of fact, he didn't look like any minister I had ever seen anywhere.

He also didn't talk like anyone I expected to hear. I was certain this man had ADHD. He was hyper. He was pouring sweat as he spoke, and he put so much energy into his speech that it wore me out just watching him.

I really couldn't figure him out. Not only did he not look like a priest, he also didn't talk like one. In fact, he spoke the language of the street—the language I and my goombahs spoke—and that immediately got my attention. It got my attention fast.

Then, when he told the class that he was a former cocaine addict, my ears flew off their hinges and flapped like an elephant.

I thought, "What is a former cocaine addict walking around with a Bible doing in a classroom in jail impersonating a priest?"

It was just blasphemy. And after listening to him some more, I thought to myself, "Either this man is crazy or I am."

But I knew he was walking out of the jail when he was done, and I was not. That answered my question.

I was confused to say the least.

I freely admit I'm confused. I'm a confused and troubled individual but at the same time...it's free! —Craig Ferguson

Initially my old, manipulative thoughts rose up again. I started thinking that I could use the dude at some point on the outside. He spoke my language. He was street smart. So I approached him after the meeting, and we quickly bonded.

But strangely enough, I began to respect him, and I found myself returning to that class weekly. I still couldn't quite figure him out, and I wanted to see what made him tick. Eventually, though, I genuinely came to like Joe (that was his name). And what he was saying began to attract my attention. Joe was a very peculiar individual, but things he said were slowly beginning to make sense to me for the first time.

It's been said that, "He who will not use the thoughts of other men's brains, proves that he has no brains of his own!"
—Charles H. Spurgeon

On one of his visits to the jail he gave me a cassette tape. (I'm clearly dating myself, here.) It contained the recording of a minister from Edison, New Jersey. His name was David T. Demola. He also didn't sound anything like a priest when he spoke. He sounded like me. And he was Italian, too. That was a big plus in my book; I could relate.

And my curiosity was intensifying.

CHAPTER 17

THE DAY THE EARTH STOOD STILL

Remember the inmate who was shadowing me and passed to me the note about that Bible study? Well, even though I was regularly attending the meetings, he was still tailing me and appeared everywhere I went. And I still wanted nothing to do with him.

One day as I was about to go up a stairway to my cell in H wing, to where I had been transferred, that guy was sitting on the catwalk to the right, on the second level, reading his Bible. I wanted to go to my cell, which was on the left. But to get to it I had to walk fairly close to him—too close to him for my comfort.

I proceeded up the metal stairs to go to the second tier. And as I stared resolutely to the left to avoid any eye contact with him, my feet suddenly turned to the right. I walked straight over to him like a robot and said, "What are you reading?"

I looked around and said to myself, "Did you say that, you fool?"

I couldn't resist. It was as if someone or something had spoken for me. My head said, "No; go to the left." But my feet wouldn't listen. My mind said, "Shut up." But my mouth wouldn't obey. I actually felt like a ventriloquist's puppet.

I bent down in squat position as he began to read to me and explain to me what he was reading. He read about the man named Jesus. He said He died for my sins.

I said, "Oh . . . What a shame."

"Sins? What is a sin?", I thought.

To be honest with you, I humored the dude because I didn't understand anything at all he was talking about. I didn't even know who that Jesus guy was. And besides, what sins could he have been talking about? As far as I knew I hadn't committed any sins.

I knew of the name; everybody has heard of the name, *Jesus Christ*. I thought he was a fictional character whose name you used only when you were either very angry, very disappointed, or when you cursed. I was completely ignorant of anything more than that.

But by that time my curiosity was starting to eat me up.

He then began to explain my sins to me, who Jesus was, and what He did for me on the cross. Then he asked, "Do you want this?"

"Want what?" I replied.

"Forgiveness", he answered.

I replied. "Why not? Sounds good. Will He get me out of jail? Will this dude Jesus pay my fines?"

I decided that I could sure use a lot of forgiveness. But I didn't know if this God, or anyone else for that matter, would be willing to forgive my laundry list of sins. I had done some pretty bad things and hurt many people in my life.

Then he followed me over to my cell, and right in front of the door, he grabbed my hands and said, "Repeat after me."

Now just a minute.

First of all, I didn't want any man holding my hands, especially in a jail cell. I didn't know what that guy might be up to. Believe me, there are too many Bible-toting weirdos in the prison system, and one learns not to trust any of the other prisoners—especially the ones who want to hold your hands. If anyone saw us, I was afraid they would think I was gay, and that didn't fly with me.

But I felt something strange that I had never felt before when he grabbed my hands. I sensed a peace unlike any peace I had ever known anytime in my life. Suddenly, the world around me disappeared, and we were the only two people on the planet. And I wasn't high on heroin.

God not only sends special angels into our lives, but sometimes He even sends them back again if we forget to take notes the first time! —Eileen Elias Freeman

Then he said, again, "Repeat after me."

And I said, "Why? By the way, do I have to sign any papers?"

He wanted me to put my trust in someone I didn't know, the person named Jesus, but I agreed to repeat after him everything he wanted me to say.

I didn't comprehend everything I was saying, and I really didn't understand completely what I was doing; but my body felt like it was floating. The feeling I got—just from repeating his words—put a heroin high to shame. It literally felt like it had to be the greatest high I ever experienced. And I thought nothing could ever top heroin.

The hair on my arms stood straight up, and I experienced peace that I never could have thought possible, and such that I could never adequately explain.

"With this kind of high, who needs heroin?" I decided.

That day was April 13th, 1987, and it was the day the earth stood still . . . for me.

And I lived happily ever after.

The End.

No . . . wait! No, no. Whoa, baby!

Now let's not get way ahead of ourselves.

Don't begin celebrating the end of my journey, yet. Don't get too happy. Things weren't as simple as that. My heart may have been changed—it really was—but I didn't say all my problems were solved that day. And I didn't say anything about getting my head on straight. What was going on in my head was a problem long before I said that prayer. And my head was still a problem after I prayed. My head was messed up big time.

But now there was a big difference between my heart and my head which would prove very difficult. They were out of synch. Now I had a new conscience that had to be answered to. And I didn't like that.

So the great battle begins. The battle between the head and the heart. The battle between good and evil. My heart was now thinking better things while my head was still full of evil thoughts...

Because of the confusion going on within me, the battle became so severe that I began to suffer with migraine headaches. The battle was going on within me.

I never had a problem with immorality, now all of a sudden I did.

I never had a problem with lying and stealing and manipulating, now all of a sudden I did.

I never had a problem looking at or pursuing any female, married or single, now all of a sudden I did.

What in the world has happened to me?

"Aha, aha! I know. I was right all along. I really did crack up! They'll send me to the Vroom Building in Trenton."

Yes, there really is a Vroom building in Trenton. It's the maximum security building in the grounds of the Trenton State Hospital, also known as the New Jersey Lunatic Asylum. The Vroom building is where the worst of the wackos are kept.

I battled those thoughts day after day, night after night. I knew something had drastically changed in my life, but it was so sudden, so profound, that it caused me great inner turmoil.

I called my sister to tell her what had happened. I wanted to tell her that I prayed to this guy named Jesus—the full effects of which I still didn't fully understand. I thought the good news would change her heart toward me; but when she heard my voice talking, she immediately slammed the phone down the same as always.

"So where is the change?" I wondered. "How come everyone doesn't love me now?"

Okay, okay, let's be realistic. What fool will automatically, all of a sudden, believe and trust the *master of manipulation?*

Then I thought and remembered, "Oh yes, I robbed her house twice. And I really did a masterful job of it."

You see, what I did was disguise myself as a handyman painting her porch while she was out. Then little by little, like a skilled surgeon (with the neighbors watching, mind you), I removed her porch window in broad daylight, slipped in, grabbed the booty, slipped out, put the window back, continued painting for ten more minutes, and called it a day.

> The thief, as will become apparent, was a special type of thief. This thief was an artist of theft. Other thieves merely stole everything that was not nailed down, but this thief stole the nails as well.
> —Terry Pratchett

My sister was seething with anger after years of me stealing from her and lying to her, and after her being manipulated by yours truly.

I kept trying to contact her. I shouted out my daughter's name at the instant she picked up the phone. "Tiffani!" But my sister slammed the phone down every time she heard my voice. DYFS (Division of Youth and Family Services—renamed Department of Children and Families in 2013) had awarded my sister custody of Tiffani, whom I hadn't seen in months.

However, finally Arleen, my sister, picked up the phone after I persistently kept calling her, and she listened to me for a while. With fire still coming out of my end of the phone, I explained to her what had happened.

Like she was going to believe me . . . Rigggggght! Oh well, I realized it would take time.

Holding on to anger is like grasping a hot coal with the intent of throwing it at someone else; you are the one who gets burned.
—Buddha

As time passed—and after several meetings with my probation officer—the detainer placed on me by the Probation Department was lifted, and bail was reinstated for me. I had no doubt that my release was orchestrated by the State Police Task Force, who wanted to tail me in hopes of me leading them to la famiglia.

I was granted a bail of ten percent. That is, ten percent of the original bail of $200,000, pending trial. The bookies put up the bail for me. Finally, I made bail. Finally I heard the guard shout out the coveted acronym, "ETG!" Everything was, indeed, To Go.

But where exactly should I go? Back to Brooklyn? That's what I had previously and cunningly planned before this God shook my life with those words, "It's Me." My head said, "Back to Brooklyn," but my heart said, "No."

So I packed what little belongings I had and gave all my chocolate to jail mates (which was customary). Then I called my newfound friend, my sister, to come pick me up—yes, my sister finally opened up to me.

I had given up hope of walking out of that prison. I had even planned at one time to escape. But there I was, walking out of jail right in front of all the guards. I loved the feeling. They no longer had control over me.

I was free!

My adjustment to life out of jail was difficult. I entered jail as an emaciated, 145 pound, strung-out, heroin-and-cocaine freak. And I left as a drug-free 185 pound, changed person. However, please do not give the jail any credit for rehabilitation.

> *Adversities such as being homeless and going to prison has made many people stronger.* —Philip Emeagwali

My sister had her brother back, and she was thrilled. And I was glad to be in her good graces. But the one person I wanted to be back with the most was my daughter, Tiffani, whom I loved so much.

Tiffani was four years old then, and she was a beautiful little angel with long strawberry-blonde, wavy hair down to her waist. She loved her daddy all through the tumultuous and dangerous days. But it had been months since I had seen her, and I didn't look quite the same. I feared she would not recognize me.

I was about to be reunited with my daughter after all those months away from her. We had no communication at all during that time. Finally, I walked into my sister's house for the first time since I burglarized it. It felt strange, especially since it was the first time I went there drug-free.

Arleen brought Tiffani out of her bedroom and said, "Guess who is here. Your daddy!"

I called her name. "Tiffani! Tiffani!" I shouted at the top of my lungs!

I expected my little girl to come running into my arms like you see in the movies, but no, she hesitated. She was afraid of me, and she backed up into my sister's skirt, holding onto her legs.

It broke my heart, but I couldn't blame her. After all, I looked more than a little strange, and she hadn't seen me like that. If you had seen me then, you would understand. I would have scared off a pack of rabid Pit Bulls. I had a hairdo that attracted any bird nearby interested in mating. I sported an Afro that would have put Jimmy Hendricks and Angela Davis to shame.

I suppose I sometimes used to act like I wasn't a human being... Sometimes I look back at myself and remember things I used to say, or my hairstyle, and I cringe. —Madonna

But my sister kept saying, "It's Daddy. It's Daddy!"

Finally, Tiffani recognized me. She ran down the hall and flew into my arms. I'll never forget that moment. The moment is etched in my memory forever. My baby daughter was finally with me once again. It was so wonderful, and so surreal at the same time.

I will never forget the day I turned Tiffani over to my sister by the expressway in Brooklyn. I thought I would never see her again, but I once again held my daughter in my arms.

I wish at this point I could end this story and tell you that "Everyone lived happily ever after"—like the ending of a 1930's Hollywood love story.

But I cannot.

I wanted to begin a new life, one like I had never known. I was back with family, and I was learning how to be a better father and care for Tiffani in a manner she deserved. I wanted that to last forever. But my mind still wasn't cooperating.

As much as I tried to dismiss it, and as much as I wanted it to be gone, something demanded my attention. It was pulling on me. My mind had to be renewed, and I was trying. But it was not taking place quickly enough. As much as I tried to fight it, thoughts of heroin continued to dominate my mind.

King Heroin was calling me back.

The war was on. My heart battled my mind daily. I remained at my sister's house and tried desperately to keep myself occupied. But the tug-of-war was becoming incessant, and my old, warped thinking was winning out.

Being on parole, I remained under the observation of the State Police. And I knew they were watching me closer than most because they wanted the mob bosses. But I had a great sense of smell. I could smell a cop at five-hundred yards, and I thought I could outsmart them.

My mind was burdened with the thought of Susan being back in Brooklyn and still heavily addicted. "How can I not go and rescue her?" I told myself. "Look at me, comfortable and drug-free. And she's back in Brooklyn months after the accident, selling her body again."

"But how can someone with a damaged mind set out to rescue anyone from a drug-infested area?" I thought. "That's like expecting Frankenstein to be a boy scout."

According to my bail agreement, I was not to leave the State of New Jersey. But my willpower was weakening bit by bit. One day I heard a train whistle. It reminded me that my sister lived only three blocks from a North Jersey Coast Line station, where I could easily catch a New York-bound train.

I frequently rode the trains to New York in the past to pick up my drugs. Temptation was overpowering me. It was as if the whistle on the train was Satan himself whistling to me, calling me.

> *Ever notice that the whisper of temptation can be heard farther than the loudest call to duty?* —Earl Wilson

I went into somewhat of a trance and told my sister, "I'm going to 7-Eleven to get a pack of cigarettes; I'll be right back."

She was a great sister, but she was naïve as a kitten curiously looking into a meat grinder. She had no street smarts at all. So she believed me, and I headed in the direction of the 7-Eleven. But I had my sights set on the train station.

I knew I shouldn't be going because my heart had been strangely changed, and it kept telling me not to go. In fact, my conscience was screaming, "Don't go! Don't go!"

But being the butt-head that I was, I ignored my heart and listened to my screwed-up head. And I quickly arrived at the train station. I looked south down the tracks. The heat was rising in waves off of the hot track-bed on that dog-day afternoon in August 1987.

I stood there trying to see if I could spot a train coming in the distance. I didn't see one, so I waited there by the track. As I impatiently waited there, a homeless, disheveled, urine-soaked man approached me and said, "Would you please go and get me something to eat."

If my heart had not been changed I would have simply told him "Buzz off, you bum." But in that encounter I suddenly discovered that I had a genuine conscience—something that had been missing for years. I had no idea at the time where the kindness I felt for the man came from, but I wasn't comfortable with my new-found feelings that seemed to be causing me to feel compassion for the man.

I couldn't respond to him like my brain told me to, so I told the man, "I'm sorry, I don't have any money." The truth is, I had just enough money for the train ticket and two $10 bags of heroin.

To my shocking surprise, that bum pulled out a wad of bills from his pocket and said, "That's okay, I have money. Please get two sandwiches, one for me and one for you."

I assume you're anticipating what was going through my mind. My brain told me, "Grab the money from this sucker and bolt." And that is what any heroin addict would do without any further thought.

But I was confused. My head was telling me that I was still a heroin addict, but I didn't feel like one any more.

As I thought about actually doing that good deed for the man (imagine that), I looked down the tracks and saw a train coming. I knew if I missed that train I would have to wait another hour, and it was getting late. I also knew that the later it was when a person got to Brooklyn, the less chance he would have of copping quality heroin.

I didn't know what to do. I actually had compassion for that guy. It was a weird feeling. It was alien to me. If I were the same person as before in a situation like that, I would have knocked him out and robbed him blind. Heroin addicts look for easy targets, and that man was holding out to me a gift that was just asking to be unwrapped.

I again glanced down the tracks toward the arriving train. And moments later I submitted to my head, hopped on the train, and headed for New York.

But you must give me a little credit; I didn't rob the man. Believe me, that was a major victory in itself. It was becoming more and more evident that I was no longer the same heroin addict. Something really had drastically changed, and I was beginning to believe it. Nevertheless, I was still addicted and potentially dangerous.

I looked at the time and saw it was getting close to 4:00 p.m.. That was not good. I knew the habits of the dealers in Brooklyn. My dealer did not sell his dope at night. My heart kept telling me to turn around and go back, but my head was determined to go on. I wanted dope. The train was a local train, and it stopped at every station.

I was getting impatient.

"Am I going to make it to Brooklyn in time? I haven't been there in months. How do I know my dealer is still in business? Or even if he's still alive? But all I have to do is locate Susan, and she will hook me up with some smoking dope."

Suddenly: Bang. Crash. Bang. Clank. Clank. Clank. Screeeeeeeech!

"What in the world is that?" I wondered in surprise as a shockwave reverberated down the length of the train. "What in the world is that?"

The train suddenly came to a standstill just outside Newark Penn Station—the last stop before entering the tunnel to New York. Everyone was frightened and asking questions. "What happened! What's going on?"

Vandals had taken a huge, loose rail and placed it across the tracks. The train hit it and derailed. I had been traveling trains for many years, and never once had anything even remotely similar to that ever happened to me.

I stared blankly for a moment, and then almost wondered out loud, "Could this be that God again?"

Oh, no! Could this be that God again trying to stop me from getting to my destination like He prevented me from getting released from jail during those thirteen days of coincidences several months ago? Am I entering the Twilight Zone again?

> *Yes, you see, there's no such thing as coincidence. There are no accidents in life. Everything that happens is the result of a calculated move that leads us to where we are.*
>
> —J. M. Darhower

I was angry. I wanted to get back to Brooklyn and see all my cohorts. And of course I had to get there to rescue Susan. I didn't even know if she was still alive. People die often in the ghettos. And their deaths don't make it into the obituaries, much less the *Daily News*. They were junkies. Who cares about a junkie other than the junkie's mother? And sometimes that's even questionable if she's a junkie too.

After we sat there motionless for hours, another train finally pulled up next to our disabled train. All of the passengers unloaded one by one and transferred to the other train beside us as it waited there before taking us to our expected destination. It was 6:00 p.m., and I was all the more determined to get my well-deserved high.

CHAPTER 18

FINDING DORY

Finally, I was out of Jersey and arriving at New York City's Penn Station. I ran to catch the C train (a subway train) and make my way to Brooklyn. After arriving in Brooklyn I exited at the elevated roadway and ran—and I mean ran—to the flag pole on Columbia Street, in the central plaza outside the entrance to the projects. That's where the dealers congregated.

It turned out that my main dealer was still in business, but he had just left.

"@#%$#@#$! Just missed him. Now what?"

"Susan, I have to find Susan!"

Susan had a strange way of getting lost in no less a way than "Dory" in the Walt Disney/Pixar film, *Finding Dory*. She would venture off in a confused state, and we couldn't find her. Finding Susan was always a challenge.

I hadn't seen Susan yet, and I was determined to get high after all the frustration I had just experienced. So I copped a bag of dope from another dealer—but I knew it was a "beat" (bad) bag.

I took my $10 bag of heroin, paid another two dollars for a spike (syringe), and made it to the same shooting gallery I had been getting high in for years. I knocked on the door. The addicts on the inside looked through the peep hole to make sure it wasn't a Swat team.

The door flew open. "Richie!" they all said. "You're back!"

I was also known by that name on the streets. It was the name given to me by la famiglia.

"Richie! Where the %$@!you been bro?"

"I did a skid bid in Jersey," I replied. On the street that means: I was locked up for a short time out of state.

But I was back home. I was home. Or was I?

I sat down, tore open a bag of heroin, and put it in the cooker (a bottle cap). I simply proceeded to do what I had done over and over, daily, during many years of addiction.

I took the spike in my hand, drew up water, and shot it into the cooker. I cooked the heroin until it had all dissolved. I then put a little piece of cotton into the liquid and drew up the heroin solution into the syringe. I turned the syringe upside down and snapped it several times with my finger to shake the bubbles loose (just like you see nurses do in the hospital).

I then pushed the plunger up to get all the air out. You know, a bubble in your blood stream can kill you. Addicts aren't stupid! Oh yeah, I was worried about the bubbles killing me, but not the heroin. Talk about stupid.

I was sitting in my chair and ready to shoot up. I crossed my legs like I had done thousands of times before. I then *tied up* (put a belt around my arm as a tourniquet to bring the veins out). I was ready at that moment to do what came natural to me. It was my lifestyle for years.

But suddenly, I paused and I looked around the room. And the strangest thing occurred as I scanned the room with my eyes. I looked at the people all around me. They were the familiar people with whom I got high for years. They were still the only people my mind felt comfortable with. They were my compadres.

I looked around the room again and then said to myself, "I don't belong here any longer. I don't belong here anymore."

I was deeply confused.

If confusion is the first step to knowledge, I must be a genius.
—Larry Leissner

Confused? Yes. But I continued doing what I was used to doing. I tapped the vein to bring it out. And I injected the syringe with a clean entry into the vein—I drew back on the syringe to make sure I hit it—and then shot the heroin into my body.

I quickly became nauseated. That was crazy to me. Shooting-up never made me sick. Nausea? I never got sick from dope like some others do. Never. Never! My body was rejecting it for the first time ever.

I couldn't understand what was happening.

"Was the dope bad? Why do I feel uncomfortable here with the same people I've always felt comfortable with in the past?" I knew something had changed, but I still had no understanding about how or why that change was taking place.

I became angry. I went through all that trouble to get here, and I didn't get high.

I was furious. And when a heroin addict doesn't get satisfied, he becomes dangerous. He is going to get more dope one way or another. He will do whatever he has to do to get his high.

The battle between my head and my heart had become a *War of the Worlds* within me. I knew Susan had to be in the vicinity, so I started looking for *Dory*. I searched and searched for her and asked everyone I could find if they had seen her. After several hours of looking I was getting closer. And finally, there she was. I found her.

By then my thoughts about rescuing Susan had disappeared from my head. We hooked up again, and she led me to Flatbush, to a friend's house, where the heroin was flowing.

Keep in mind that I had told my sister I was going to 7-Eleven to get cigarettes. I told her I would be back shortly. She knew something had happened when I didn't return within thirty minutes. One day became three days. Days turned into a week—

then two weeks. Susan and I were still in Flatbush, staying at the house belonging to the couple who lived there. And I was getting high again, daily.

For two weeks I was hiding out in Flatbush, and I thought nobody knew where I was. The only person I contacted during those two weeks was my sister, and I told her some wild, fantasy story that she, surprisingly, believed. But I never told her where I was.

One day the phone rang early in the morning. Tony, my friend, said it was for me.

"It's for me?" I asked, completely confused.

"It's for you."

I took the telephone receiver and put it up to my ear. I couldn't believe what I heard when the person on the other end of the line began speaking. Believe it or not, it was Trooper T. of the New Jersey State Police. He had tracked me down.

I always thought I could outsmart the police. But I found out something different. The police are always one step ahead of a dumb drug addict.

"But how did he get this number?"

I found out the answer. They had my sister's phone tapped all along. They were monitoring my movement and all telephone calls hoping I would contact la famiglia in Brooklyn.

The trooper threatened that if I didn't return to Jersey immediately, they would be on their way to get me. So I went back to Jersey, but Susan returned to Red Hook. I told her I would be back again to get her. And I did return. I returned again and again. I continued to get high, but every time I did, I was violating my conscience. I knew this God was watching me wherever I went. I really got shook up one day when I walked past a Catholic church and saw one of the Sisters staring out the door at me. I actually ran. I was scared to death.

I was convinced that a bolt of lightning was going to come down from heaven and put me out of my misery. I knew I couldn't hide from Him. After all, didn't that God find me in the Monmouth County Correctional Institution?

"If he found me in MCCI, and if He found me in Red Hook, He can find me anywhere," I thought.

Nevertheless, I couldn't stop. I kept returning to Brooklyn over and over again. I wanted to bring Susan back with me, but she was afraid of being separated from her source of heroin. And I couldn't overcome the addiction. It was just too strong. It was too powerful, much stronger than I was. My head was clearly winning the battle over the heart.

I looked up from where I was, and it all seemed hopeless again.

In an age of hope men looked up at the night sky and saw "the heavens." In an age of hopelessness, they call it simply "space." Emptiness has replaced fullness.
—Peter Kreeft

Again Susan and I soon fell into deeply depraved living. She started selling her body again, and this time I became her pimp. I hated it though. Day after day, night after night, we continued in that existence.

I found myself walking through the streets of Brooklyn, crying out to the God I didn't really know or understand, "Please kill me, please kill me! I don't want to do these things any more, but I can't stop. Please kill me. I know you're watching me, and I still can't stop. Please, please kill me!"

And I meant it. I was sincere. I wanted Him to kill me.

The weeks continued on, one after another. With fifteen bucks in my pocket from a trick Susan had just turned, she and I were on our way to pick up cocaine from Cuba (not the country; it was the name of the dealer, pronounced "Kooba").

But as we walked I began feeling like . . . I felt like my heart was telling me . . . that if we picked up and shot up the speedballs we planned, we would surely die. I felt a compulsion to leave New York, and do it right away.

We arrived at the corner where Cuba was dealing to pick up *pedico* (Spanish street slang for cocaine). And it was just then that I heard that voice again. It was clear to me. It was the same voice I heard while I was in jail. That same voice spoke to my heart again, but there on the street the voice had a dire message for me.

"If you do not leave Brooklyn now, you will die."

I knew that voice. I knew we had to leave. We had only fifteen dollars. It was enough to buy either the pedico or tickets to Jersey.

I thought about the consequences of returning to New Jersey. I had once again destroyed my relationship with my sister, and there was no way at all she would allow Susan anywhere near her house.

But a strange strength came over me. A determination rose up in me that I couldn't understand. I left his street corner, and began walking toward the subway station, repeating over and over to Susan as I walked, "If we don't leave now we are going to die. If we don't leave now we are going to die."

Susan followed me ten yards behind, cursing me all along the way. "We have nowhere to go. Are you crazy? #@%$#$%#$!. Can't you see it's hopeless? It's hopeless!"

When you say a situation or a person is hopeless, you are slamming the door in the face of God. —Charles L. Allen

I said back to her, "I know, but we have to go, and we have to go now!"

She followed me, cursing like a banshee. "You're crazy, you %*@#$! ^$#@*&*! Where will we go?"

I kept repeating, "We have to leave now! We have to leave right now!"

I didn't know where the strength came from to enable me to take such a strong and firm stand with her—much less to gain and retain the sanity that all of a sudden I was displaying. But if I were to guess, I would say it came from that God, who seemed to be following me wherever I went.

Susan really had no choice but to follow me. I was her sugar daddy. So she followed me, even though she continued cursing me out like a truck driver running late.

At one point she raced up in front of me, crazed, and spit on the sidewalk in front of me to provoke me to stop. She knew how much I despised that. I cursed her out but even that didn't move me from my determination to leave.

With Susan trailing behind, we finally made it to Penn Station, boarded a train to Jersey, and headed to Belmar, where my sister lived. One hour and forty five minutes later we pulled into Belmar station.

There we were, dirty and wet, since it was raining. We arrived there with all our earthly possessions—the clothes on our backs and only enough heroin to keep us straight until we could make local connections and enter a rehab, or get into a methadone program.

We arrived at midnight. We stood there alone at the train station, in the rain, with nowhere to go. And to add insult to injury, Susan had pneumonia. She was sick and coughed continually.

But instead of giving up, we made it to the Belmar Marina about a quarter mile away and broke into the cabin of a boat to get out of the wind and the weather. When you are desperate, you do what you've got to do. I was afraid Susan was going to die of pneumonia.

It was cold in the boat there in the Marina, but it was shelter. Early in the morning, just as the sun rose, I shook Susan awake and told her we had to leave before the fishermen came and discovered us. If we didn't leave we would have been arrested for trespassing and breaking and entering.

"What should I do? Where should I go?" I thought.

I knew I had to take a chance at my sister's. I had no choice. I was still pretty good at breaking and entering (ahem . . . even if I do say so myself), so I put my street skills to work once again. I picked the rear door lock of her house,and we made our way into her small back porch. We lay down on the floor and passed out.

Slam! We were suddenly awakened in a daze. A door slammed shut, and standing there was my sister, with steam coming from her nostrils. She looked like Goliath in a gladiator ring staring down at a midget.

"What the hell are you two doing here?" She said, forcefully. "Get the hell out of my house! Now!"

Rejected and depressed, weak and still wet—and with Susan still coughing—we grabbed our shoes and stumbled toward the door.

Then suddenly, and to our amazement, she said, "STOP! I can't send you out like an animal. You'll die."

Now I have to tell you, my sister was one of those who called themselves "born-again" Christians.

> *Human beings, like plants, grow in the soil of acceptance, not in the atmosphere of rejection.* —John Powell

She permitted us to stay for a few days, but not without some very strong boundaries, and rightly so. Our boundaries were the four-by-six-foot rear section of the porch where the dog stayed. The dog moved out, and we moved in. We were not allowed in the house. I could certainly understand that. Why should she trust me? Because I told her I had a spiritual awakening in jail? My actions up to then had not proven that true very well.

Nevertheless, Susan and I were happy that we had a roof over our heads and warmth. Considering what we had been through, and how we were used to living—in the shooting galleries and abandoned, filthy houses of Red Hook—the back porch was like an executive suite at the Omni Berkshire in Manhattan.

After several days, and with a little strength returning to us, Arleen wanted us to be productive and keep our minds occupied. So she put me to work around the house and paid me. Paying me was dumb—dumb, dumb, dumb. I told you she was not street-smart.

There is a cardinal rule when dealing with people struggling with drug addiction: never put money in their hands. Never violate that rule, especially when dealing with a heroin addict. It's like giving a loaded gun to a six-year-old and saying don't point it at the cat.

I was still very physically weak from the many years of addiction that took a toll on my body, but I wanted the money. One project my sister gave me was to put a swing set together in the back yard for my young nephews.

Have you ever seen the directions for putting together a children's swing set? It's like putting together the Milky Way Galaxy! My mind was in no condition to create. But I pushed myself, completed it, and earned fifty dollars. Not good. Not good.

I've already established that my heart was changing. But my actions also showed that my head was not. And remember, there had been no spiritual awakening in Susan yet—not a glimmer. She just wanted drugs, and when we were together, temptation always won out.

Both of us still wanted to get high. And all we needed was a trigger—a way to initiate the action. The fifty dollars Arleen gave me for my work was that trigger, and I pulled it.

I began to scheme and manipulate as usual. I never lost any of those technical skills.

After all we went through, escaping from New York, we started all over again. But this time, right under the nose of my sister on the back porch of her house.

As long as you continue to manipulate, you will never be fit for success in life. God is determined to strip us of all confidence in self, leaving us with total confidence in Him.

—Don Wilkerson from "My Postings"

I made some local connections for drugs. That's easy for an addict to do. Familiar spirits attract familiar spirits. I could smell another addict from within a ten-mile radius. (It was either mental telepathy or a spiritual connection with evil.) I simply cruised the locally-known drug area, and, sure enough, the demons showed up in full force as soon as they sensed my presence.

Nevertheless, the war continued within me. The daily battles between good and evil had me exhausted. I didn't enjoy the drugs anymore, even though I still craved them. My heart was no longer participating in what I was doing, but that demon heroin still had a powerful stronghold on my mind.

With Susan in an even deeper addiction than I, it was hopeless for either of us to get free of drugs as long as we remained together. We were our own worst enemies. And I finally convinced her that we would never escape without help. For us, one foot was already in the grave.

Even in the grave, all is not lost.   —Edgar Allan Poe

I talked to certain individuals who had been in drug treatment centers and was told of a residential program in South Jersey. Susan did not want to go, but I told her it was our only hope. She was afraid to leave and enter into an unfamiliar environment. But to my surprise, Susan agreed to it.

I confessed to my sister and told her that we had thought we were free from the drugs but fell again into serious abuse.

None are more hopelessly enslaved than those who falsely believe they are free. —Johann Wolfgang von Goethe

We asked Arleen for help, and she agreed to drive us to South Jersey so Susan could enter the program. The director of the program set an intake date for Susan on the coming Thursday. It was Monday, so she was to enter the program in only three days. It was Susan's best hope. It was our only hope. I knew we had to separate. Addicts feed on each other. We were like poison to each other.

Then it happened. We looked at each other, and heroin, that demon, whispered into our ears, "Go back to Brooklyn for just one more high with me before she enters the program, just one more last moment with me."

CHAPTER 19

ONE MORE HIGH

Everything in my heart shouted, "No, don't go!" But the temptation was too strong for me. I was losing another battle in my war. My head ruled. I couldn't overcome and resist the call of heroin.

But I knew something bad was going to happen. I could sense it. I was turning my ear away from that voice that was continually saying, "Do not Go! Do not go!"

Wednesday came, the day before Susan was going to leave to enter the program. And that day we hopped on a train and left for Brooklyn for just one more high. After arriving it was no time at all until we were back in our shooting gallery on Columbia Avenue in Red Hook, where we had wasted so many years of our lives.

> *Just cause you got the monkey off your back doesn't mean the circus has left town.*
> —George Carlin

But the same voice that spoke to me in the county jail cell—the voice of the same God who seemed to want to show me He could control my destiny—was still clearly telling me, "Stop. Don't do it!"

I felt powerless to deny the pull I felt to get high with Susan again, but I knew something life-threatening was going to happen if I ignored the warning.

Thoughts of danger and death—those things never bothered me before. For years we lived daily on the edge of both. Death didn't concern or frighten us. Then why was the thought of those things so strong in my heart? Susan and I had suffered and survived many overdoses and near overdoses, but we just figured that to be a part of our lifestyle.

If we died, we died.

Susan was susceptible to seizures from heroin and cocaine speedballs, and she had suffered many close calls with them in the past. Her seizures were frightening, not to her (since she was unconscious), but to me. I watched her go through those seizures, and I could do nothing about them. I felt helpless.

When she seized, she twisted and foamed at the mouth like an eel out of water on a boat deck.

If you died, you died.

Que sera, sera. Whatever will be, will be.

Just part of the game.

But this time and for the first time in 25 years, something was different. I wanted to live. Profoundly different. I didn't understand it, but this desire to have life was slowly growing stronger.

There's that "Voice" again. "Don't Go." Repeated again and again. I was confused. Deeply confused. I was powerless. Like a desperately hungry man being drawn to food, we were drawn back to Brooklyn.

> *Addiction is a dependence on a behavior or substance that a person is powerless to stop.* —Encyclopedia.com

We quickly picked up several bags of heroin and cocaine (speedballs) from Cuba, yes Cuba. Remember him, he was still in business.

The stamp or tape on those glassine bags was put on the bags to identify the dealer and the quality of the drug. Cuba had green tape on his bags. We knew Cuba personally, and we knew he had good dope. We knew he didn't try to beat anyone (sell bad dope).

Susan and I made our way back to the shooting gallery and shot up for what was supposed to be the one last time to get high together before she entered the program. As the cocaine and heroin entered our veins and raced to our minds, the rush silenced my ears to any voice of safety.

Of course the demon lied again. He said one more time. But that was not enough to satisfy either him or us. For as quickly as the rush came, it was gone; and we hungered for more.

Any addict will tell you that once a person starts shooting speedballs in the evening, the only way to stop shooting is to run out of money, get busted by the cops, or overdose. No addict has the will to stop, so it was inevitable that one of those things was going to happen to us that night. Those are your options.

> *Cocaine isn't habit forming. I should know–I've been using it for years.* —Tallulah Bankhead

So we went down to the corner again to Cuba. He still had the green tape we were looking for. Again, we knew it was safe. It was not beat or cut with rat poison. Yes—rat poison. Some low-lifes cut their drugs with rat poison.

They don't care if it kills you. They don't care who lives or dies. All they care about is the money.

But we were street-smart, right? We knew better than to buy such junk.

We returned back to the gallery and shot up. Now the craving continued to increase and the hold on our bodies and minds was like a vice, driving us back to the streets again and again.

But by the fourth time we went to the corner we were too late. Cuba had already gone for the night. We were desperate and out of control.

> *Desperation is like stealing from the Mafia: you stand a good chance of attracting the wrong attention.* —Douglas Horton

We had to have more speedballs. We wandered around there until we spotted someone else dealing drugs. And he also had green tape.

We went up to him and said "This is Cuba's dope, right?"

He said, "Si, this is Cuba's."

The best pitch I ever heard about cocaine was back in the early eighties when a street dealer followed me down the sidewalk going: I got some great blow man. I got the stuff that killed Belushi.
       —Denis Leary

But it wasn't Cuba's. The counterfeits came out when Cuba left the street corner. And we knew that; we were street smart, right? But like I said, we were desperate. So we took a chance like so many other times. It's all part of the game. We knew we were taking a risk.

We copped his speedball and returned to the gallery.

We frantically put the dope in the cooker as if we were being driven by a force. Yes, and it was a force; it was the force of a paralyzing addiction. We cooked the dope until it completely dissolved, dropped in the cotton, and drew up the liquid into the syringe.

Susan was in the bathroom with someone helping her to get a hit, and I was in the bedroom. Susan was a daredevil. She always banged the speedballs (which means she injected it all with one quick thrust). She was crazy.

She always wanted the maximum rush. I always "booted" (shot a little, pulled back, shot a little, pulled back) then banged the rest. It was safer that way.

I got a hit first, I booted very little at first, though, because I didn't trust that green tape.

Immediately my body jolted as if I had just grabbed onto a live power line. I convulsed. My head flashed and began to pound. I quickly screamed out to Susan.

"DON'T SHOOT IT! DON'T SHOOT IT! IT'S POISON! IT'S POISON!"

But I was too late. She banged the entire bag, and she immediately went into uncontrollable convulsions. Her body twisted and convulsed violently. I screamed for them to carry her into the bedroom where I was. She was unconscious as they laid her down on the bed. And of course no one called a doctor or 911.

I'll never forget that moment because it is the moment that changed my life forever.

All the other addicts in the shooting gallery simply stood around the bed, emotionless, with syringes sticking from their arms, and watched her deep, labored breaths become slower and slower, then more shallow with each one, then farther and farther apart.

Then she took her last breath.

One addict, who was standing there watching the spectacle, said, "She's dead". He and the others showed no emotions. Life and death meant nothing in a shooting gallery. It was just a spectacle for them. I'll never forget that picture in my mind of that evening.

I remembered the "Voice" saying, "Don't go, something terrible is going to happen".

Then my whole life flashed in front of me in a micro second. I was on my knees looking over Susan at the base of the bed. I saw both our lives end at that moment—not just hers, but mine too. I could see no future for me. Susan and I ran out of time, and I blamed myself. I thought of suicide.

It is always consoling to think of suicide: in that way one gets through many a bad night.   —Friedrich Nietzsche

Suddenly I experienced total silence and solitude in the midst of that wild shooting gallery. It was as if I were the only person there. I heard nothing but an eerie silence. I called out to this God I was running from. I pleaded with Him.

"Please God, please," I pleaded. "I know I don't really know you, but please don't let her die!"

"We were so close. So close. Please don't let her die. We tried. We really did. We were so close. I'm sorry. I'm sorry. You know she was supposed to enter the program in the morning. But now she is dead. Please don't let her die! We were so close."

I wouldn't let go and continued to plead for God's mercy. But she lay there for a long time with no breathing and no other sign of life.

Suddenly, without any artificial respiration, without anyone pounding on her chest, and without paramedics, her body convulsed once more, and she took a loud, deep, agonizing breath.

"Uhhhhhhhhhhh!"

Even though I had been begging God not to let her die, I was in disbelief. Frozen—I couldn't believe what I was seeing. I was stunned, as were all the other drug addicts in the room. She began to breathe, and her breathing slowly became more steady and calm. Then I began talking to her and trying to bring her back. In total amazement to all of us she slowly regained consciousness.

Susan was alive. She was weak and shaky, but alive. She slowly regained her strength, and she was able to walk by morning.

There is no way on earth Susan should have survived the poisoned dope. And for that matter, there is no earthly explanation for why I wasn't sickened by even the small amount of it I took. Something supernatural happened that night.

But the power of heroin laced speedballs overruled the human will to live even after this near death experience. This powerful stronghold of heroin and cocaine on the mind was pulling us back to our deaths.

We were both weakening fast, and our minds were entertaining a return to the streets.

A heroin addict can be said to have a death wish. I can't explain it. He arrogantly flirts with death—staring at death eye to eye and almost challenging it to a fatal game, saying, "Who will win?"

But I knew we had to run or we would lose the game. I knew we had to run, and run quickly, back to Jersey, where Susan must enter the drug program. We were given a second chance.

Finally, and for the first time, my heart won a battle. It overruled my head, but not without an intense fight. Addiction is powerful. Only an addict can truly understand its power. I grabbed her by the hand, and we ran to the subway. We made it to the train and returned to Jersey . . . alive!

The following day, my sister took us to South Jersey, and Susan entered the residential program there. Victory!

Victory? Not quite so fast.

We experienced a huge victory that day. But of course it was clearly only a partial victory; for there was still one other person who needed to be dealt with . . . me.

And I was a difficult case. I was still struggling with having a new heart but old thinking. Still disillusioned and confused, I was fighting my temptation for drugs. I was fighting it every moment of every day.

I needed help, too. But that help needed to come from people who could understand what I was going through. My sister? No. She tried, but there's no way she could fully understand what I was going through. But who then? It had to be someone who had struggled with an addiction and found victory. A person like that would be the one who could both understand and help me.

I had to stay occupied, busy. I had to become reacquainted with the more wholesome part of society. I didn't belong to the underworld any longer, and I no longer wanted to live in the darkness. I had to be retrained to function responsibly. But regardless of where I got help, or who provided the help I needed, it was not going to be an easy task.

I felt like the task of restoring me to what most people would classify as a normal acting and thinking person would be similar to teaching someone who awoke from a twenty-five year coma—and from actually being brain-dead for twenty-five years—how to talk, how to function in a changed world, and how to relate to others in a civilized and acceptable manner.

> *I want to feel passion, I want to feel pain. I want to weep at the sound of your name. Come make me laugh, come make me cry... just make me feel alive.* —Joey Lauren Adams

Of the things that I needed to re-learn, I believe the hardest for me was to learn once again how to relate to others in a civilized manner. It was hard for me to trust people after twenty-five years in the world of organized crime and drug addiction on the tough streets of Brooklyn and Harlem. I found it hard to trust anyone.

My first response to being challenged in any way was to respond quickly with violence and a foul mouth. It was survival of the fittest on those streets. I always had to be prepared for confrontation.

Even after so many years have now passed—to this very day—I still walk with a stiff right arm out of habit as if I were still holding the knife hidden in my sleeve.

The road to rehabilitation is a long one.

CHAPTER 20

BETWEEN A ROCK AND A HARD PLACE

I needed a mentor. I needed someone to be a living example for me. And one man emerged to become the mentor I needed. It was Joe, the same Joe who taught the Bible study when I was incarcerated.

I maintained contact with Joe after getting out of prison. He could relate to me, and he was used in a great way to steer me back into society. I trusted that man, and he became an important part of my life.

Joe knew that I needed to be kept busy. He knew that while Susan was away in the program I also needed to be rehabilitated. So Joe offered me a job.

"You mean a job where they take out taxes? A job that makes me get up every morning at the same time? Early?"

—and I took it because I trusted him. I hadn't worked a "real" job in twenty-five years. But I trusted Joe, so I took it.

I had no skills other than carpentry from the days before my addiction, but he found a job for me working at the same company where he worked. He was the supervisor of a fine crystal importer warehouse, and he offered me the honorable position of a packer. That's right, a packer. I worked in a packing line and packed boxes. Day in and day out I packed boxes of crystal glasses, vases, plates, and other things.

In time I actually began to like the job. Nevertheless, even while my mind was occupied, and while I was being mentored by a great guy, my mind would constantly drift back to heroin. That demon never wants to let go. The thirst I had for drugs was always there, waiting for a trigger to set it off. And there are many "triggers" that will set off an addict who is recovering. The most powerful trigger is, yes, you guessed it, MONEY.

As I said earlier, money should never be put in the hands of one who is still struggling from heroin addiction. But guess what? I had a job. And guess what? Every week was payday. And you know what that meant, right? You guessed it.

Every Friday evening my head was on the train back to New York along with my arms, legs, and torso—and of course, my paycheck. I didn't want to go. I was fighting a valiant fight. And I was winning some battles now and then; but the war was far from over. I was fighting a powerful demon. There were still many battles with my mind ahead for me.

Drugs are a bet with your mind. —Jim Morrison

Every Friday, week after week, I was back in Brooklyn and hating myself for it. I still lived with my sister, and I lied over and over to Arleen as to where I was going and what I was doing. It was common for me to bring heroin back to the house with me and shoot it in my little room. (Yes, I was still on the back porch).

And it wasn't unusual for me to still be high on Monday morning when I reported to Joe at the warehouse. I never told him, and he never knew. (He knows now.)

Nevertheless, I continued to work, getting high only on the weekends, and dealing with minor withdrawal symptoms. Each Monday morning I suffered from a "Chippy" (a mild form of withdrawal). By Tuesday night, though, the "monkey" was gone. One learned to live with "Chippys" if you had to.

Heroin quickly subdues the body and mind. Nevertheless, I continued to go to work.

One Friday, Joe asked me if I would be interested in going to church with him, and I respectfully declined. After all, I thought I might meet that God who knocked me down in jail. And I was still afraid of Him. But mostly, I declined because I felt my past would be exposed. And I thought the people there would look down on me. I still felt dirty. I still felt like a dirty junkie.

Joe asked me again the following week. He never pressured me, he just asked again, and I declined again.

Joe asked me again the third week, and because I liked him so much, I thought I would do him a favor and go one time with him. But I have to admit, I also felt I owed this God for the miracle. I could never forget how He saved Susan the day she overdosed, and how He answered my desperate prayer.

I thought I owed it to God to go to church that one time.

So I agreed to go with him, and we decided to meet that evening at Dunkin Donuts, where I changed my clothes in the bathroom after work. I waited for him to pick me up there, and it seemed strange to me because it was not Sunday. It was a Thursday evening service.

"Huh, I always thought church was a Sunday thing."

Joe arrived to pick me up at six o'clock. I came out of the donut shop, got in his car, and we were off. I noticed he had a big grin on his face. That was because he knew what I was about to experience, but I had no clue why he was smiling at the time.

We traveled about forty-five minutes to Edison, New Jersey. We went down Oak Tree Road and hit a traffic jam. I said to myself, "Good! There must be an accident up ahead. Maybe I won't have to go now."

Well, fool me, it soon became evident that the traffic jam was not caused by an accident. It was caused by the long line of cars trying to get into the parking lot at Joe's church. I scratched my head.

"Why would so many people be going to church, and on a Thursday night to boot? There must be a wedding. That's it, a wedding."

We finally pulled up to a building, and I asked Joe, "Where's the church?"

I expected to see a tall white steeple and hear the bell ringing. That's what I thought a church is supposed to look like. But that building looked more like the warehouse I worked in. And I wondered where all the people wearing their suits and ties to attend the wedding were. Isn't that the proper way people go to a wedding at a church?

I was confused. But Joe didn't say much. He just sat there grinning from ear to ear.

We parked the car and finally made our way through hundreds of people who looked strangely like me. (And that was frightening.)

Black, white, brown, Asian. Strangely enough, the same similar people that I hung out with in Brooklyn. I just couldn't figure this out. This must be a very special wedding.

No, no wedding? It was church. "Just church," he explained.

We entered the doors after being greeted by dozens of people with big smiles and who were reaching out to hug me.

"Get away from me. Are you kidding? I don't play that stuff. This is one strange church," I said to myself.

I quickly followed Joe as we made our way through a sea of people to a couple of seats about seven rows back from the front. I sat there stunned. And Joe sat there with that big silly grin still painted all over his face.

"Well, now", I thought, "aren't the hymns about to begin? If I'm not mistaken, I remember one called *Blessed Assurance*. Maybe they'll sing that one. I won't feel so strange because I can at least lip sync. Okay, here we go."

I folded my hands in reverence and was ready for the priest to walk out when all of a sudden a young man who looked like a rock star came to the center stage with a guitar strapped over his shoulder. I looked around to be absolutely sure I was in a church. Then all of a sudden . . .

Bang! Bang! Bang!

I instantly and instinctively ducked. I thought I was back in Red Hook. "Relax, no guns being fired," I thought. "It's only the drummer."

I was dazed. Instead of *Blessed Assurance*, they began singing something about stepping on the devil's head, and about the devil being under our feet. So I looked to see if he was under my feet, too.

Everybody stood up and raised both hands. Now *that* I felt comfortable with. I was used to "assuming the position" during an arrest. It came natural, so I raised my hands with them. I flashed back to what it was like when I was busted.

Then all of a sudden they began to sing louder, they began to dance, and they began to shout.

They're doing this stuff in church?

I couldn't believe what I was experiencing. It may have been crazy to me, but they were sure happy about it. I was left with my mouth wide open.

And Joe was still grinning.

He never said a word to me. He just kept grinning.

Well, I thought they would get worn out after a couple of songs, and we would sit down. Rigggggght! They were still singing and shouting close to an hour later.

I never saw anything like it in my life. They were happy. And strangely, regardless of how foreign it all was to me, I wanted to be that happy, too.

Then the singing enveloped me. It was furry and resonant, coming from everyone's very heart. There was no sense of performance or judgment, only that the music was breath and food.
—Anne Lamott

But I didn't have a clue of what was going on. Jumping, dancing, shouting. Why? I didn't understand it. What exactly were they so happy about anyway?

And then the strangest thing happened. A man walked up to the platform, took the microphone, and started speaking in a very strange way. Whatever he was saying, he was saying it in a language I had never heard before. At that point I really wanted to excuse myself. I told myself it must be some kind of cult activity. But curiosity kept me in my seat to see what was coming next.

Then I was about to be in for the greatest shock of all. In walked a small dark, Italian man, mustache and all. His name was Pastor David T. Demola. He was an Italian! And he had a healthy head of black hair.

"Hey, I have a healthy head of black hair!" He also had a big black mustache. "Say, I have a big black mustache." He was an Italian from Staten Island. "And what do you know, I'm Italian and a born New Yorker."

Okay, where is the priest? Pastor Demola must have come out to introduce the priest—you know, the man with the stiff collar and the stern, straight face of judgment. Isn't that what ministers look like? Well, maybe some, but not at Faith Fellowship. (That was the name of the church.)

Faith Fellowship—to me that was a strange name for a church. I thought all churches were named something like St. Francis of Assisi, Mt. Carmel, Sisters of the Sacred Heart, or some other religious name like that.

Ask me if I was confused.

And to confuse me even more, Pastor Demola was not there to introduce anyone. He was the "priest" of the church! Whooo!

Well, I can tell you, that man captured my attention. I could relate to him. He had more energy than a square mile of solar cells. And to my greatest surprise, his voice sounded familiar. Where did I hear that voice before?

Ahhh, the county jail! That's right, the county jail.

He was the man on the tape that was given to me by Joe himself. What a coincidence! It was the same man. The same pastor. The man on the tape. I was overwhelmed. To me, I was meeting a celebrity!

He then began to speak. He spoke in a fashion I could understand. His delivery was down to earth. He spoke words that I could relate to. That was cool. I began to like that place because it wasn't like a church.

And guess what! Joe was still grinning.

That was the first time I went to Faith Fellowship, but it certainly was not the last. A love affair had begun for me. That was in the summer of 1987.

I have to say that I was speechless on the way home with Joe, and I was really tired. I had just been at a three hour long church service. Three hours! Are you serious? That's more time spent inside a church all at once than I had spent inside churches in my entire life. Wow! Many new things were happening for me.

Going to church, working steadily—all of that was new for me. And to tell you the truth, I was getting to like it.

But what wasn't new to me was the continuing struggle that was still going on inside me. Even though I was attending church and holding down a job, I couldn't find the freedom I was looking for. I still didn't have freedom from the influence of the demon of heroin.

I continued to go to church week after week, and week after week I continued to go back to New York to get high on each payday. The frustration was building because I still had no peace. I wanted to have that inner happiness like the rest of the people in that church; but I had that war still going on inside of me that no one knew about. The wrestling match between my new heart and my old head continued, and I just couldn't take it any longer.

Even at times during the weekdays I conned my sister or her friends to take me somewhere to fulfill some fictitious request. While they waited for me in their car, I picked up some heroin to take back to the house. Over and over, day after day, even after such a big change in my life, I couldn't escape the heroin.

I was becoming extremely depressed inside, and was nearly ready to give up again.

One of those days when I picked up heroin locally with the unwitting assistance of my sister was on a weekend, a Saturday during the summer. I went into the bathroom at my sister's house, the favorite hiding place for addicts, and tied-up as I prepared to shoot my dope. I heard laughter and looked toward the small bathroom window.

I peered out to see Arleen and all her friends having a barbecue. They were laughing and having fun in the backyard. I turned my head away while struggling to find a vein so I could get my hit. I heard more laughter from outside, and I felt more frustration inside. With all of that, I blew the shot. I missed the vein. Furious and frustrated, I broke.

That time I just broke.

I ran in to the living room, fell to my knees, and said to God, "If I have to live one more day like this I want to die!"

I've said that before, but I meant it. That time I meant it. The war inside me was over. It was over. I gave up. I was at wit's end. There was no fight left in me. I had finally come to the end of myself. Disgusted, I lay down and passed out.

The weekend went by, and I went to work at the warehouse as I had been doing for several months. Monday, Tuesday, and Wednesday passed. Thursday came, and I was in church that night. Then it was payday again.

At 5:00 p.m. that Friday, like every other Friday before, the paychecks were handed out. My usual pattern on Friday evening was to hop on the bus and go straight to New York for my weekend high. But that Friday was not just another typical Friday.

I had been outside, and a co-worker met me at the corner across the street from the warehouse to give me my check. He extended his hand with the paycheck in it. I reached out and took it. Then, at the very moment I received my check and held it in my hand that day, I heard that voice again.

I heard that same voice, and this time the voice said, "It's over. It's over."

And I knew at that very moment the battle was over. I was free! I knew it! Inside me, I knew it!

I was finally free!

I remembered my plea to God that previous Saturday—when I was at my wit's end—when I said "If I have to live one more day like this I want to die." Well, instead of allowing me to die, God met me and brought a miracle with Him when I needed it most. He met me at my wit's end.

I was free, and it felt like an eight-hundred-pound gorilla had been lifted off my back. I felt such an overwhelming joy inside of me that I could hardly contain myself.

We can only appreciate the miracle of a sunrise if we have waited in the darkness.   —Unknown

But beyond that, believe it or not, a silly grin—like the one on Joe's face—began to form on my face too. And it slowly became a permanent fixture. That's what happens when a person is delivered from a heroin addiction. When a person is delivered supernaturally, they are delivered! They are D-E-L-I-V-E-R-E-D.

It's not like in AA or NA (and I thank God for those programs), where one is "recovering." A person may be *recovering* for fifty years, but never to really experience the freedom associated with deliverance, the ultimate freedom. When God delivers you, you are delivered. You are free.

After that day I had a song in that new heart my brain was always fighting with. And I began to develop as a man. I began to enjoy church and started to finally understand what Pastor David Demola was teaching.

I continued to work with Joe. And after that day there were two silly grins in the warehouse. I was happy and content, and I even began saving money. Things were definitely looking up . . . at least for me.

Susan was still in the program in South Jersey, and she was still battling her demon. That remained daily on my mind.

Nevertheless, months went by, and I continued to be strengthened. My mind was able to ward off the flirtations of heroin for the first time in twenty-five years. I finally had the fortitude to isolate myself from former associations with the wrong people. I was being restored more and more. I was becoming whole.

My concern then turned to my legal matters. All through that time, I was still out on bail. And I had a court sentencing date coming up soon.

"I'm clearly a different person now," I considered. "I have no conscious desire for heroin any longer. I've broken off all association with the mob. They can't put me back in jail! Can they?" The prospect of going back to jail was a real concern for me, but ahead of me was yet another miracle.

I was facing a possible five to seven years in jail, minimum, for drug charges since I was a repeat offender—and especially since

I had been connected to organized crime. My court date arrived, and I stood before the judge. But unlike my experiences so many times before, the judge sentenced me to five years' probation, not incarceration.

That time, I was not led out of the court room in handcuffs. Was it God? Was it a good lawyer? Or both, perhaps? I don't know. But one thing I did know was that I had my life back—a normal life!

(Slow down.) Not so fast, man. Little did I know that there were others who still wanted a piece of that life—like for instance, the State of New Jersey and a few former drug dealers I had beat in the past for some money. But that is another story.

CHAPTER 21

GOODBYE HEROIN

Being in Jersey without a driver's license is like being a cowboy on the range in Montana without a horse. A person can do just fine without a car in New York City, but a person is helpless in Jersey without a vehicle.

Okay, a driver's license. But what state in their right mind would give this man a driver's license?

I had collected more Motor Vehicle tickets in New York than Barnum and Bailey collected at the gate of their opening day circus at Madison Square Garden. I had more accidents (happening almost daily), more careless driving tickets, and more parking tickets than anyone I knew.

My traffic record surely made me a strong candidate for *The Guinness Book of World Records*. I think I still may be able to win the prized distinction for the most tickets based on my past record. I had thousands of dollars-worth of traffic tickets. My license was not only revoked in New York, the last I heard it had also been revoked everywhere in the Milky Way Galaxy!

> *Reckless automobile driving arouses the suspicion that much of the horse sense of the good old days was possessed by the horse.* —Unknown

Brace yourself for this. So I went down to New Jersey Motor Vehicles in Trenton, ready to get down on my knees and beg and sob, kick and scratch, to plead with them. I asked if there was some way for me to get a conditional, hardship license.

They entered my name in their computer, and lo-and-behold, my name came up clean. That's right, completely clean with no records. Another miracle.

I immediately double-checked to see if I was really who I thought I was. I looked in the mirror. Yup, it was me alright. And they were telling *me*—the world record ticket holder—that *I* had a clean record?

I waved my hand in front of the face of the attendant to see if he was awake. Sure enough he was awake and alive.

So I didn't pursue the subject any further. I just said calmly, "I would like to apply for a driver's license." And the rest is history.

I later found out that 1987 was a transitional year regarding computer systems (new software) between New York and New Jersey Motor Vehicles in which they both began working together sharing information on traffic offenders.

Prior to that year, whatever motor vehicle violation you received in a particular state was confined to that state.

But in 1987 New York and New Jersey, and possibly other states, began working together where penalties from either state were being honored on both sides of the border.

The miracle is that my New York driving violations record was never transferred during the software transitional period. Lost in cyberspace? Miracle? You decide.

All of my New York insane driving records never reached the Jersey computers. And all my violations were in New York.

A miracle ... I think so. Susan's very similar driving record was transferred to Jersey. She never drove a car again.

So, I'm back on the road again.

This time, however, I had brakes and a license.

You know, somebody actually complimented me on my driving today. They left a little note on the windscreen, it said "Parking Fine."
                                                    —Tommy Cooper

One of the first things I wanted to do after getting my license was to go see Susan. I had to visit her to see how she was doing, but I was hesitant. What do I say? Is she still struggling? In spite of my reservations, though, I went to see her. I borrowed my sister's car (can you believe that?) and left for South Jersey.

By that time Susan had completed the first phase of the program and been taken into a halfway house. It was managed by a married couple who appeared to be responsible, straight individuals, and who helped certain people transition back into society.

I took Tiffani and my son, Ron, with me to visit Susan. We arrived at the house, and everything appeared to be fine. We sat down in their living room and had some cold drinks. It was a hot summer day.

Suddenly, I realized there was no one around besides us as I, Tiffani, and Ron sat alone there in the living room. Everyone else had disappeared. So we waited, and we waited, and we waited.

Then Susan finally appeared and said that John, the husband, wanted to see me. I asked where he was. Susan said "upstairs in the third floor attic."

So I left Tiffani with my son and went up there, clueless about what was going on. And, wham! When I arrived they all were standing in a circle there in the attic passing around a hash pipe and kief, a powerful form of marijuana. It caught me off guard. Something like that was the farthest thing from my thoughts.

John said to me, come take a hit. I was stunned because I was clean. I was a new creature. No more drugs for me!

Rigggght!

I refused, and then I refused again when he offered it to me the second time. But he persisted, and I began to weaken. I didn't want to get involved, but I discovered that I was not as strong yet as I thought. And I joined them for a "harmless hit."

By now you should be fully convinced that there is no such thing as a "harmless hit" of anything. I think I've already demonstrated that pretty well in my story up to now, but here is a reminder.

I knew it was stupid, but I did it anyway. I failed again. I failed myself again!

Stupidity is also a gift of God, but one mustn't misuse it.
— Pope John Paul II

Now keep in mind, that wasn't just any old, run-of-the-mill kind of marijuana. It was high-quality kief. It wasn't the kind grandma used to grow in the backyard garden. And to top it off, it was laced with hallucinogens. And hallucinogens were something I could never handle.

All of a sudden I went down, flat on my back in the middle of the floor. I lay there staring straight up, hating myself, frozen, and asking myself, "Why? Why, why, why did I allow myself to fall into this trap again?!"

I thought I was delivered from this addictive nature. Well, yes, I was, but not from the old habits. The only way to find total victory is to get my mind renewed. That is a process. Right? Not surgery. Although a lobotomy was not a bad idea at this point.

I got to thinking about relationships and partial lobotomies. Two seemingly different ideas that might just be perfect together—like chocolate and peanut butter.
— Sarah Jessica Parker

So there I was, lying prostrate on my back as if I had been nailed down on the floor. I couldn't move. I couldn't talk. All I could do was think to myself.

"Please God, make this go away. I will never do this again. I have to drive my kids home. I don't want them to see this, and I can't even stand up. Please help me!"

Slowly my head stopped spinning, and I was able to stand. I was still shaky and in a complete stupor as I went down the stairs. I got to the living room, and I said, "Kids, let's get out of here."

I put them in the car, and barely being able to sit up straight, I drove very slowly half dazed all the way home.

> *Have you ever noticed that anybody driving slower than you is an idiot, and anyone going faster than you is a maniac?*
> —George Carlin

Much to my dismay, I had to leave Susan there that day. I had no choice. I wanted to get Susan out of that house, but my sister wasn't ready for us to stay together again at her house. I discussed the dilemma with Arleen, and the only solution was for us to get a temporary room somewhere to rent.

We weren't ready to live alone, but Arleen didn't understand that. She didn't know that I had once again slipped and gotten high. And I didn't tell her that Susan was living with potheads. Shortly afterwards I returned to South Jersey to remove Susan from that house.

I didn't have a lot of money, so Susan and I had few options when it came to where we could go. But I was willing to live just about anywhere to get her away from those two weirdos. We soon found ourselves living in one of the rooms in a drug-infested motel. Trapped again.

We were isolated without transportation or money and relegated to living once again in a bad environment. So where could we go? We had nowhere else to go and no one to turn to.

And moving in there was just another of our bad decisions.

Some choices we live not only once but a thousand times over, remembering them for the rest of our lives. —Richard Bach

Sure enough, Susan and I both were once again quickly exposed to sexual immorality and heroin. We were falling fast. We felt dirty. But that time we cried out for help. And our cries were heard.

After several weeks in that forsaken motel we were rescued by family and friends. After they saw our boat sinking, they relocated us and started monitoring us. We could not do it on our own. We needed help, or we would have slipped back into the underworld again—probably for the final time.

Not long after that, I was back working with Joe (who was still grinning). And Susan soon began working again as a hairdresser after a long, long, long, hiatus from that profession.

I wish I could tell you how Susan and I finally found peace, love, and healing together after that. I wish I could relate to you how Susan and I were finally able to conquer life together, beat all the odds. But I can't.

As much as we tried, Susan and I couldn't make it together. We couldn't. The wounds were too deep to heal. Too much damage had been done to our emotions and feelings. And when it comes right down to it, we did not know how to communicate with each other in the real world—only in the underworld.

The memories were too painful. But we valiantly tried. In spite of our efforts, though, we permanently parted ways two years later followed by a divorce. And after seemingly endless court battles, we found ourselves with joint custody of Tiffani after she was restored to us by the courts.

The path toward restoration on which I was walking was long, sometimes extremely challenging, and painful. But I continued attending church with Joe, and I eventually even became a member. I also continued to work hard in the warehouse with him, and little by little I began to trust God.

I'm sad to say, though, that Susan continued abusing heroin for years in a continuous on-going struggle with her addictive nature. She could not separate herself from the influences of her environment. Susan was eventually incarcerated for possession of heroin and prostitution; and after more court battles, I was awarded sole and permanent custody of my Tiffani.

Believe it or not, I raised Tiffani as a single dad. I even put her through private school straight through high school by the grace of God and the help of a wonderful couple who became my mother and father.

Susan and I had very little contact over the following years, but we remained civil toward one another. There was a soul-tie between us that couldn't be broken, yet it was not possible for us to discover a viable relationship as she continued to live a double life.

I broke free. But unfortunately, though, not everyone does.

When I think about those who haven't made it out of heroin addiction, I think of Hannah Meredith, a young lady from Llanelli, South Wales. When Hannah was seventeen, she already had been addicted to heroin for two and a half years. She came to understand the devastating effects of her addiction, and she wrote a letter about it.

I always think of Susan when I read Hannah Meredith's heartbreaking "Letter to Heroin". They even were similar in appearance.

GOODBYE HEROIN / by 17-year-old Hannah Meredith

The letter she penned was addressed, "Dear Heroin."

Dear Heroin

I never want to touch you ever again, you've ruined my life, made me steal from my family, on probation 'cause of you, why I choose you I don't know?

You're the worst thing that ever came into my life. Yes, I did love you but now it's time to say goodbye.

I'm so ashamed of myself 'cause of you. I OD three times, you're a big risk to anyone that does it and to me.

So I'm going to be strong and stay away from you and never touch you again. My family have supported me all the way but I just kick them up the backside taking advantage of them.

Stole off my mother, granddad, Mam Iscoed. I borrowed money off her and didn't give it back. She's getting old now, and look what you've made me do, to my nan—£120 stolen off her, once again 'cause of you.

I love my family from the bottom of my heart, it's not nice being called a junkie or 'smack ed'.

It feels horrible, you feel so small. Well I feel small, you made me feel like I'm worth nothing, just a dirty junkie sticking needles in my arms.

You're out of my life now, don't need you no more.

Yeah, you've messed me up nearly two and a half years of my life but I've still got my whole life ahead of me and I'm going to prove to everyone that I can stay away from you, going to college, getting a job and a car.

Then get on with my life and get my family's trust back. Stop offending, that's the only reason I was doing all that 'cause of your dirty addiction. You make me sick to be honest with you.

I did love the buzz of you but you're not worth it. By losing my family, thinking about you p****s me off.

But not anymore, I'll make sure you stay away from me, and I'll stay away from you. I was brought up by a good family not a bad one, yeah I've had a lot of problems in my life, been quite bad actually, all because of you (Heroin) (gear), (smack)!!

You're a killer, you've killed a lot of people and really they are good people. I'm lucky that you haven't put me in Box Cemetery. Lost loads of my mates and it hurts me, they sometimes blank me 'cause they know I've been on you (gear) it's not nice when I've got pin holes in my arms and marks, track marks.

The illness that I go through when I use you and the after effects, cold turkey, clucking (corr), withdrawals, it's the worst feeling that you've put me through, being bad off you.

Wanted to kill myself a few times 'cause I couldn't go through it. Well guess what (heroin) I can and did do it. I can beat you anytime. I can control you, you don't control me.

I've got enough will power to get you out of my life for good. I'm strong and much stronger than you can ever be. I'm not losing anything over you. Goodbye heroin.

Never again. Family comes first. —*Hannah Meredith*

Hannah Meredith, from Llanelli, South Wales, died of an overdose of Heroin on October 20, 2009 just weeks away from her 18th birthday.

—Hannah Meredith Foundation (HMF)
 https://www.facebook.com/hannahmeredithfoundation

Hannah didn't make it.

My heart is broken for Hannah, as well as Justin P., who died at the age of twenty two. There was Paul I., who overdosed at twenty-three. But there are also thousands more who overdose and die every year from this demon from hell named King Heroin.

I realize that my name should have been included on the list of those whose lives have been ended in tragedy by their addictions. Call it "survivor's guilt," perhaps, but my feelings over that has left an imprint on my soul that will never go away.

Heroin is a cancer, but it is one that no earthly physician, chemotherapy, or radiation treatment can cure. If heroin is not *spiritually* eradicated from an addict's life, it will seek out occasion to rear its ugly head again and again. It keeps saying, "I own you now. I own your mind, I own your body."

I have found that only the King of Heaven can truly dethrone the King of Heroin from his position of power, where one can confidently say, "It's over, It's over, I'm free".

King Heroin is no longer king over my life. He had me on the ropes for many years. I lost many battles. He had me near death. But he lost the war. I may have failed many times. But I've learned in life that our acts of failing do not ultimately define us as failures unless we give up.

I said earlier there is no easy way out of heroin addiction, and that is true, but there is a way.

ONE WAY to be free from the addictive nature. And that is through surrender to God.

> *The greatness of man's power is the measure of his surrender.*
> —William Booth

My heart aches for Hannah. For although I never met her, in my heart I knew her torment intimately and personally, and that's because we shared the same demon. When any of the Hannahs of this world die, a part of me dies with each one.

I have three beautiful daughters today, and I can think of nothing more devastating, more heartbreaking, than to see a precious daughter—anyone's daughter—enslaved to heroin. It robs their souls. It robs their dignity. It robs them of their potential. It robs their beauty. And finally, it robs them of their dreams.

A cemetery is the richest place on earth, It is where all the dreams and visions die —Myles Munroe

---

I too have written a personal letter to Heroin.

Goodbye, Heroin

Oh Heroin, how I once loved you, and how I believed you loved me. How I lived for you, but you betrayed me—as you did Hannah, Justin, Paul, and so many others.

You are selfish, you only take from others and give nothing but empty promises in return. How many more will you deceive, how many more will you promise peace but give them pain? How many more families will you destroy?

God created you in another form to do good, but you turned to evil. How many lives and limbs did your father save on the battlefields of war, only to deceive them later with your hunger for souls?

You almost took me with you; you had me on the brink of death so many times, but you couldn't succeed. You failed. You lost. I was rescued by ONE much more powerful than you— much more.

I will fight you. I will fight you for the rest of my life.

You lose Heroin; you lose!

CHAPTER 22

HOPE AGAINST HOPE

To hope against hope simply means to have hope even when the situation appears to be hopeless.

Unfortunately many will allow their dreams and visions to pass them by even if they survive heroin. Because if heroin doesn't kill you, it will surely rob your potential to live a full quality life.

Jimmie Jack, a dear friend and founder of Long Island Teen Challenge, a faith based drug rehabilitation center, wrote a book entitled, "I Can Dream Again", after many years of hopelessness trapped in drug addiction as I was.

It would serve you well to read his book as well.

It all begins with hope.

The following is an edited excerpt from a message given in Albany New York by Don Wilkerson, co-founder of Times

Square Church and Teen Challenge (by permission).

For over 45 years there has been a so called war on drugs.

The war is over.

Not because it's been won—but because unfortunately drug abuse has become an accepted reality.

We live in a drug saturated society Just watch T.V. commercials. Here we find what I call,"Prime Time Pushers".

We've become a society of drug users.

When people ask me what is the first thing a person must have to begin the process towards freedom from heroin,

I say, "You got to have hope."

*It's possible to live some 40 days without food; about 7 without water; & just some minutes without air—but you can't live a moment without **hope**.*

What do you give an addict?

You give them Hope...

Hope is like the sun, which, as we journey toward it, casts the shadow of our burden behind us. Samuel Smiles

Some say you can't change a person who does not want to change. And that may be true!

But if you've been told it's not possible to change ...then why bother?...

But God is waiting at Wit's End for any addict who finds his way there.

(Portions edited and revised by permission)

I have said before—*There is no easy way out of addiction.*

BUT there is a way out.

Obviously I, (the author), speak from experience. My credentials are the tracks that have been carved as permanent scars into my arms as reminders from years of abuse.

That was my belief and my attitude for 25 years.

"Ronn, get help"!! "Ronn, you are dying"!!

My response, "What's the use? There's no way out."

Yes, That may be true for some.

But I found my way to Wit's End.

Nobody can go back and start a new beginning, but anyone can start today and make a new ending.

—Maria Robinson, former addict

Those tracks on my arms to this day daily remind me of those dark hopeless days. But most of all, they remind me of that "Voice" that rescued me, the "Voice" that gave me hope.

I don't go to Brooklyn any longer to "cop" drugs; I now go to Brooklyn to "cop" Pizza. And while I'm there I reflect on how God gave me the ability to break free from the Underworld.

Nothing gets a real Italian more angry than Pizza Hut.

—Anonymous

It was now 1992.

I was single and I was lonely. And I was vulnerable. Although delivered from the 25 years of battle with heroin, another demon remembered my very first weakness. The female gender.

And along came a woman of American Indian decent. Beautiful. So beautiful. Sooooooooooooooo beautiful. My eyes locked on her like David's eyes locked on Bathsheba.

A whole new set of challenges—or shall I say temptations, now entered my life.

This intriguing woman became my Delilah. So we will call her Delilah.

An affection which is not inspired by the Lord will soon be transformed into lust. Samson is not alone in the history of man in failing in this regard. Delilah is still cutting the hair of men today.
—Watchman Nee

My Delilah seduced me one night in no less a way than Samson's Delilah seduced him. Except my Delilah didn't cut my hair. Must I say more. I was powerless. I made Samson look like a saint. At least he was sleeping.

This led to a marriage stamped "Made in hell". It began in hell and it ended in 1999 after 7 years of hell.

This was a marriage many tried to discourage me from making. But I was smitten. I was addicted. She had a spell over me. I was "sleeping with the enemy."

I wouldn't listen.

I have an angel on one shoulder, and a devil on the other. I'm also deaf in one ear.
—Pinterest

So as I was struggling with an old familiar addiction—a Delilah addiction, in my life, Susan continued dangerously to date the demon of heroin.

I had said earlier, not everyone makes it.

The following years for Susan were a constant struggle of desperately trying to break free from the influence of heroin and opiates that surrounded her, but there was simply no more fight left in her. She was too weak.

Susan no longer returned to the streets of New York.

She would no longer spit in the gutters of Brooklyn ever again.

After her release from jail she continued to flirt with heroin and returned to the streets of the Jersey shore.

Hannah didn't make it.

Susan didn't make it.

Susan miraculously reached 53 years of age. She was saved from herself. She was her own worst enemy. I prepared Tiffani our daughter many times to expect this day to come.

After escaping death numerous times with the 9 lives of a cat, that day sadly came. It was like a part of me had died. A part of my heart suddenly was missing. I felt guilty. I survived.

We had all been in a war together in the Underworld. The three of us.

Could I have done more to help her? I do not know.

Susan valiantly battled King Heroin, but she battled him alone. You cannot battle him alone. He will win. He won. I sobbed.

Tiffani and I together alone silently placed a headstone to mark where her ashes lie. Then we walked away silently, never saying a word to each other. There were no words. Only silence spoke.

I will never forget Susan and how we suffered together and how we struggled together to survive in our addictions. Did we ever really love each other? I am not sure. Genuine love does not exist in the Underworld. It is simply a dependency. But there was a powerful soul bond between us.

There were even some good times, rare as they were before the demon took control and stole them from us. I will try to remember them.

Nevertheless, there is good news.

Today Tiffani is the wonderful mother of 3 sons in a strong marriage.

As for me. I was not only delivered from heroin in 1987, but from Delilah in 1999. No more Delilah!!

Today I am re-married to a wonderful woman from the Philippines where we currently reside with our daughter; and continue to counsel and teach on the dangers of substance addiction.

I'm convinced the only true pathway to breaking free from King Heroin's Underworld is with God. If you are at war with King Heroin—if you are fighting him alone—you will most definitely lose. He will eventually wear you down, win your soul and take your life as he did my dear Susan.

The war continues. King Heroin doesn't give up too easy. He doesn't want to give up his throne. He is very cunning. He will masquerade in many different forms and with many different nicknames such as oxycodone, fentanyl, methadone, and suboxone. Do not trust him.

King Heroin is the same demon. The same demon from hell in all of them. True, there is no easy way to win the war with him. There is no magic wand. But there is a way.

ONE WAY.

Listen for that "Voice". That Voice that rescued me from heroin's grip. That Voice that changed my life forever.

Then your battle is won.